EX LIBRIS

PRINTED IN ITALY

BOOK OF
TRADITIONAL ENGLISH COOKERY

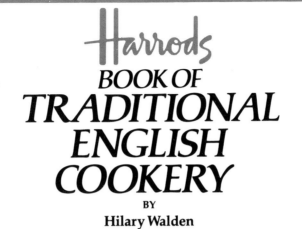

Harrods
BOOK OF
TRADITIONAL
ENGLISH
COOKERY

BY

Hilary Walden

**ARBOR
HOUSE**

NEW YORK

Published in the United States of America by
Arbor House Publishing Company
and in Canada by Fitzhenry & Whiteside Ltd
by arrangement with Ebury Press, London

———————⚫———————

EDITORS: Fiona MacIntyre, Felicity Jackson, Susan Friedland
ART DIRECTOR: Frank Phillips
DESIGNER: Marshall Art
PHOTOGRAPHY: Grant Symon
STYLIST: Sue Russell
HOME ECONOMISTS: Susanna Tee, Janet Smith and Maxine Clark

Ebury Press would like to thank Harrods, and their archivist
Margaret Baber, for allowing the use of the black and white
illustrations taken from Harrods catalogues.

Library of Congress Cataloging-in-Publication Data

Walden, Hilary.
Harrods book of traditional English cookery.

1. Cookery, British. 2. Harrods Ltd. I. Harrods Ltd.
II. Title.
TX717.W2   1986   641.5941   86-7969
ISBN 0-87795-839-4

Contents

*All eggs used in this book are
large unless otherwise stated.*

Introduction

TRADITIONAL English cooking has a rich and varied history, owing much of its character to the manor houses, rectories and well-to-do merchants' homes that have been the backbone of English society for so many years.

In the first century A.D., the Romans brought with them an interest in food, and a pride in developing new and unusual ways of preparing it. Cooking standards deteriorated somewhat after their departure – the success of a banquet became dependent upon the ravenous appetites of the assembled mass of diners and the sheer volume of food, rather than the quality of the food and the way it was cooked and presented.

The choice of food then was as varied as it is today, if somewhat different. Foods were natural and in many cases wild. In addition to the meats eaten today, the diet included wild boar, suckling pig, goat, kid and mutton, as well as any bird that could be shot, trapped or snared, such as bittern, curlew, peacock, lark, blackbird, thrush, rook and crow. Goats' and ewes' milk was drunk as well as cows' milk, and the sea, rivers and lakes were fully exploited for their abundant supplies of fish and shellfish.

They might not have had the exotic fruits from the tropics that fill supermarket shelves today, but the Briton's forebearers picked wild berries, mulberries, quinces and medlars, and used flowers, herbs and wild produce.

The journeys of the crusaders resulted in supplies of oranges, lemons, dates, prunes and other dried fruits, almonds and the spices which are such a feature of medieval cooking. It is commonly supposed that food was heavily spiced and seasoned to diguise the taint of food that was going bad, but as there was such easy access to wild food for much of the year it would have been quite unnecessary.

By Tudor and Elizabethan times, food had begun to assume much greater importance. Traders and other voyagers returned, fired with enthusiasm for the cooking they had tasted abroad, and brought back ingredients – and chefs – to re-create the dishes at their own tables. The opening of new trade routes brought different foods, not only from the East, but also from the New World – sweet potatoes from Mexico, corn, potatoes, sugars and molasses, tea, coffee and chocolate to drink.

Heavily spiced, rich foods went out of fashion under the Puritan influence of the mid-seventeenth century when pleasure in eating became unfashionable, and rich foods positively sinful. Although this severe austerity was short-lived, food generally became more simple.

The agricultural and industrial revolutions brought more changes with the emergence of a new middle class of professional men, successful traders and merchants who married into the lower nobility and aristocracy. They created new employment opportunities for the women and girls who had been driven off the land in search of work. These girls provided an abundant supply of cheap domestic labor – housemaids, kitchenmaids and cooks.

Two grades of cook soon evolved. One was the plain cook, who helped with the housework as well as providing the meals. These meals would have been very simple roasts, chops and pies, and it is from such cooks that country-style cooking began to be introduced into the diet of townspeople. The other was the "professed" cook, employed by the higher echelons of society, who did no housework. With the help of the one or two maids she was training, she catered for the everyday meals of her master and mistress, cooked for the children in the nursery, the servants, and for the special occasion dinner parties that required more elaborate food.

Entertaining was very important to the upper middle classes and aristocracy. The lengthy, showy meals given by the wealthy were designed to impress, and people vied with each other to present their tables in the most superb fashion.

The lady of the house had to extend her repertoire of dishes, so that every space on the table could be filled. This usually meant looking to foreign sources, especially France, as French cuisine was very much in vogue. French chefs who had fled the revolution in their own country were being employed in increasing numbers by the court, nobility and aristocracy. This was the age of the great names of Louis Eustace Ude, Carème and Alexis Soyer. If a chef could not be employed full-time, one would be hired for special occasions. Those lower down the social scale would hire a cook who had been trained – or at least claimed to have been – in France. Failing all else, a perfectly normal English dish would be given a French-sounding name.

By the middle of the nineteenth century, a formal dinner followed the style still used today, with soup served first, followed by fish and then meat. The sweet pies and desserts that had been served alongside the entrées joined the sweet dishes at the end of the meal.

Lunch was a less elaborate affair, consisting of something like chops or steaks, and to bridge the gap before dinner there was the new institution of afternoon tea. This coincided with the improvement in the quality of flour, a drop in the price of sugar and the development in America of an effective leavening agent in 1850.

The new society of literary, political and artistic figures at that time gathered at fashionable coffee and chocolate houses or shops, then later at gentlemen's clubs, mostly in London's St James', such as the Reform Club and Boodles. Some of the best-loved traditional dishes have emanated from these establishments. Others are associated with particular fairs or festivals, such as Michaelmas Goose, in September.

➤ REGIONAL VARIATIONS ➤

Considering the size of England, it is remarkable how varied the regional dishes are, with social class, climate, soil differences and economy of the area all affecting its food.

In the West Country of Devon and Cornwall, fish, shellfish and cream have long played an important part in the economy, and are frequent ingredients in many of the dishes of the area. In Somerset and Wiltshire, cows graze on lush pastureland and their milk is used both for cooking and making the famous Cheddar cheese. The by-product, whey, is fed to the pigs which in turn provide the local products such as faggots and sausages. Traditionally, these pork specialties also had a distinct flavor from the pigs' diet of the local apples.

The fertile Vale of Evesham is renowned for its early vegetables and fruit, asparagus, strawberries and plums, though it is the county of Kent that is known as the "garden of England," as the soil and climate are ideal for growing all manner of fruits, particularly apples, cherries and plums. It is hardly surprising that these crop up repeatedly in the local dishes.

In the midland counties of Leicestershire and Northamptonshire, pasturelands provide not only milk and beef, but cheeses such as Stilton, which in turn have led to a thriving pig industry and local pork products such as the Melton Mowbray pork pies. The long tradition of hunting in the forests in this part of England has led to the popularity of game dishes in that region.

The generally poorer northern counties, with their harsher climate, are better known for more filling and economical fare such as pan haggerty, and for their cakes and baking. Many of the traditional recipes are cooked on a griddle as that could be heated over a peat fire – the coal needed for heating an oven being more costly.

The recipes in this book have been taken from across the whole span of history from the Middle Ages. It is often very difficult to attribute them to particular regions, as a basic recipe may be found in a number of forms in different regions, with varying stories surrounding its origin.

Much of the traditional English food is fairly simple, plain and straightforward, but it does require some practical knowledge to cook a superb roast; to make feather-light, crisp pastry for pies, or delicate dumplings that melt in the mouth rather than solid lumps of dough that sink to the bottom of a stew.

Even the many slow-cooked dishes found in old recipe books must be cooked in just the right way to appreciate their full flavor and see why they have withstood the test of time. Originally these dishes were cooked in large amounts in heavy casseroles or pots beside, or suspended over, the fire in an open hearth, so the liquid never boiled to toughen and shrink the fibers of the meat – they just melted and fell apart. With modern stoves, and cooking smaller quantities, it takes more care to achieve the same slow, gentle cooking of former days.

The recipes have all been adapted to suit modern tastes, ingredients and equipment, to enable the present-day cook to experience the glory of traditional English cooking easily and with confidence.

Soups and Light Dishes

THROUGHOUT history, soups have been the stand-by, sometimes even the staple diet of the poor – the poorer the person the plainer the soup. But there is a lot more to traditional English soups than meager broths.

Inns would have large, steaming pots of soup ready to feed to travelers while they waited for their main dish of meat. In country kitchens the soup pot, full of vegetables and chunks of meat or fowl, would sit beside the fire to provide a complete meal, the well-flavored broth often being eaten first to take the edge off the appetite.

Journeys to far-away places brought spicy soups such as mulligatawny, and by Victorian times soup had become the proper way to start a meal, especially when the soup was real turtle.

Many of the dishes that we eat today as snacks or first courses have grown up from the traditions of high tea – a meal served at about six o'clock, consisting of a savory cooked dish and cake or a cold sweet pastry. Other dishes, such as kedgeree and deviled kidneys, appeared on the breakfast tables, while others, such as angels on horseback, rounded off a formal dinner.

Almond Soup

This soup, also called white soup, dates back to medieval times when almonds were used extensively in cooking. It tastes delicate and luxurious, yet is very easy and quite economical to make.

¾ cup ground almonds	lemon juice
1½ quarts chicken or light veal stock	¼ cup toasted slivered almonds, to serve
1 bay leaf	
⅔ cup heavy cream	SERVES SIX
2 egg yolks	
salt and white pepper	

Put the almonds into a saucepan and blend in the stock. Bring to a boil, stirring, then add the bay leaf and simmer for 30 minutes.

Remove the bay leaf, purée the soup in a blender or food processor, then return to a clean saucepan and reheat gently.

Blend the cream into the egg yolks in a bowl, then stir in a little of the soup. Pour back into the saucepan and heat gently, stirring, until the soup thickens. Do not allow to boil. Season with salt, pepper and lemon juice.

Serve the soup sprinkled with toasted almonds.

Apple Soup

Recipes for apple soups date from at least the fifteenth century, and they are especially common in the apple-growing regions of Kent, Somerset and Leicestershire. This particular recipe makes a light soup that is in keeping with today's eating styles.

12 oz tart apples, cored and quartered	2 cinnamon sticks
12 oz baking apples, cored and quartered	3 cloves
	¾ cup chicken stock
lemon juice, for sprinkling	¼ cup heavy cream
	¼ cup sour cream
1 cup dry hard cider	salt and white pepper

SERVES FOUR

Sprinkle one quartered baking apple with lemon juice and set aside.

Put the remaining apples, cider, cinnamon and cloves in a saucepan and bring to a boil. Cover and simmer for about 10 minutes until the apples are tender.

Remove the cinnamon and cloves, then purée the apples with the stock and creams. Reheat the soup gently, stirring, but do not allow to boil. Season.

Cut the reserved apple quarter into fine strips. Serve the soup garnished with the apple strips.

Mulligatawny Soup

This soup is of Indian origin and came into the English kitchen via the members of the army and colonial service during the nineteenth century. There are many versions of the recipe but they all have a spicy curry flavor.

4 tablespoons unsalted butter	6 black peppercorns, lightly crushed
2½ lb chicken, cut up or 6 small chicken pieces	about 1 tablespoon lemon juice
1 onion, chopped	salt and pepper
1 carrot, chopped	2 tablespoons heavy cream (optional)
1 small turnip, chopped	2 cups cooked rice and grated apple tossed in lemon juice, to serve
about 1 tablespoon curry powder	
1 quart white or brown veal stock	
4 cloves	

SERVES SIX

Melt the butter in a large saucepan, add the chicken and cook until a light even brown. Remove with a slotted spoon.

Stir the onion, carrot and turnip into the pan and cook, stirring occasionally, until lightly colored. Stir the curry powder into the vegetables and cook for 1–2 minutes. Return the chicken to the pan, stir in the stock and bring just to a boil. Cover and simmer very gently for about 1¼ hours.

Lift out the chicken, discard the skin and chop the meat. Purée the liquid and return to the rinsed out pan with the chicken. Add lemon juice and seasoning to taste, then reheat. Swirl the cream into the soup as it is served and accompany with individual bowls of cooked rice and grated apple.

Potted Shrimp

The quality of the shrimp from the Lancashire town of Morecambe has been renowned since the eighteenth century. Before the days of refrigeration, the shrimps were sealed in butter in pots to preserve them.

½ lb shelled shrimp
8 tablespoons (1 stick)
   unsalted butter, cubed
pinch of ground mace
salt and cayenne
6–8 tablespoons unsalted
   butter, melted
parsley sprigs, to garnish

thin slices of brown
   bread and lemon
   wedges, to serve

SERVES FOUR

Chop a quarter of the shrimp. Melt the cubed butter slowly, carefully skimming off any foam that rises to the surface. Stir in all the shrimp and heat gently without boiling.

Remove from the heat and stir in the mace, cayenne and a little salt. Pour into pots and leave until cold, then seal. Meanwhile, let the melted butter stand until the sediment has sunk to the bottom, then gently pour off the fat, straining it through cheesecloth. When the potted shrimp are cold seal the surface with a layer of the clarified butter dividing it equally among the pots.

Allow to set, then cover with plastic wrap and keep in the refrigerator.

Leave the potted shrimps at room temperature for about an hour before serving.

Garnish each pot with a parsley sprig and serve with thin slices of brown bread and butter and wedges of lemon.

Angels on Horseback

This was a popular savory in Victorian times when oysters were plentiful and cheap. Scallops or prunes can be used in place of oysters to make archangels or devils on horseback.

8 oysters
8 bacon slices
4 slices of toast
unsalted butter, for
   spreading

watercress, to garnish

MAKES EIGHT

Scrub the oysters with a scrubbing brush. Hold each one in a cloth in the palm of one hand, flat side uppermost, and pry open the shells at the hinge. Remove the oysters from their shells.

Wrap a slice of bacon around each oyster and place on a broiler rack with the seams underneath. Place under a hot broiler until crisp, then turn the rolls over to crisp the underside.

Cut two circles from each slice of toast and butter the circles. Place one bacon roll on each circle of toast. Garnish with a little watercress.

ALMOND SOUP (page 10)

Bacon Froise

*Froise or fraize has been mentioned in recipes
from the fifteenth century onward and probably
originally referred to the cooking of a batter-like
mixture in the hot fat that had dripped from a
roast as it cooked on a spit.*

6 tablespoons all-purpose flour	1 egg white
pepper	2 tablespoons unsalted butter
1 egg, beaten	fried wild mushrooms or
⅔ cup milk	broiled cultivated ones
4 slices bacon, cut into strips	and tomatoes, to serve

SERVES FOUR

Sift the flour into a bowl, season with pepper and
form a well in the center. Pour the egg into the well
and gradually draw in the dry ingredients then beat
in the milk, a little at a time, to give a smooth batter.
Let stand for at least an hour.

Gently cook the bacon in a non-stick frying pan
until the fat runs and the bacon is crisp. Drain on
paper towels.

Beat the egg white until stiff, but not dry and
lightly fold into the batter.

Melt the butter in the frying pan then, when
sizzling, add half the batter and spread out to cover
the bottom of the pan. Cook over a moderate heat
until the base is a light golden brown and the top is
just set. Scatter the bacon over the surface of the
batter and cover with the remaining batter. Cook
until the top is set, then turn the "cake" over and
brown the other side.

Transfer to a warmed plate and cut into wedges.
Serve accompanied by mushrooms and tomatoes.

Fricassée of Eggs

*A pretty early eighteenth century luncheon dish
that could also nowadays be served for supper.*

6 eggs, at room temperature	4 cooked artichoke bottoms, sliced
7 tablespoons unsalted butter	salt and pepper
3 tablespoons all-purpose flour	parsley sprigs or finely chopped fresh parsley, to garnish
1½ cups veal or chicken stock	crisp fried bread croûtons, to serve (optional)
1 teaspoon finely chopped fresh parsley	
1 teaspoon finely chopped fresh thyme or ½ teaspoon dried	SERVES FOUR

Simmer the eggs for 8 minutes until they are just
hard-boiled. Place immediately in cold water, then
remove the shells and cut four of the eggs into
quarters. Place in a serving dish.

Slice the other two eggs into halves and carefully
ease out the yolks. Sieve 1½ of the yolks and chop
1½ of the whites. Cut the remaining halves in half
and add to the serving dish.

Melt 3 tablespoons butter in a saucepan, stir in the
flour and cook for 2 minutes, stirring occasionally.
Gradually stir in the stock and bring to a boil,
stirring. Add the herbs and simmer for 10 minutes.

Meanwhile, melt 2 tablespoons of the butter in a
frying pan, add the artichoke slices and heat
through. Add to the sauce and season well. Over a
low heat, stir in the remaining butter.

Pour the sauce over the eggs. Garnish neatly with
sieved egg yolk, chopped white and parsley.
Arrange croûtons around the edge of the dish, if
liked, and serve immediately.

Potted Beef

Potting is a very old method of preserving whereby cooked meat or fish is hermetically sealed in butter. Potted meats are delicious for first courses, picnics or packed meals. If the sealing layer of butter is unbroken and the tops of the pots remain covered, the potted beef can be kept in the refrigerator for 2–3 weeks. Leave at room temperature for 30 minutes before serving.

1 lb lean top round of beef, cut into 1-inch cubes	3 juniper berries, crushed
	1 bay leaf
	salt
1½ cups dry white wine	2 tablespoons brandy
6 tablespoons dry Madeira	12 tablespoons (1½ sticks) unsalted butter, softened
1 cup brown stock, preferably veal	
2 cloves	
blade of mace	SERVES FOUR TO SIX
6 black peppercorns, lightly crushed	

Place the beef in a shallow ovenproof casserole. Add the wine, Madeira, stock, spices, bay leaf and salt. Cover tightly and cook in a preheated 250° oven for about 2¼ hours until very tender.

Remove the meat with a slotted spoon and let drain. Strain the stock and boil until reduced to 3 tablespoons.

Pound the meat to a paste, then work in the reduced stock, the brandy and 4 tablespoons butter.

Pack firmly into two earthenware or glass pots, making sure there are no air pockets. Gently melt the remaining butter. Skim off the foam from the surface, then spoon the clear butter over the surface of the meat, leaving the milky residue in the pan. Leave to set, then cover and leave overnight.

Scotch Woodcock

Scotch woodcock was popular in Victorian and Edwardian England as a course at the end of dinner. Nowadays, it can be served as a light first course or a tasty snack.

6 slices of bread	6 anchovy fillets, split in half lengthwise and soaked in a little milk, then drained
4 tablespoons unsalted butter	
4 egg yolks	
1¼ cups heavy cream	parsley sprigs, to garnish
pepper and cayenne	
Gentleman's Relish or anchovy paste, for spreading	SERVES SIX

Toast the bread. Meanwhile, melt the butter in a heavy-based saucepan over a low heat.

Blend the egg yolks with the cream, stir into the butter and heat gently, stirring with a wooden spoon until the mixture just begins to thicken. It will continue to cook after it has been removed from the heat. Do not allow to boil. Season with black pepper and cayenne.

Cut a large circle from each slice of toast and spread with Gentleman's Relish or anchovy paste. Divide the cream mixture between the toast circles. Lay two pieces of anchovy on each serving and garnish with parsley.

Kedgeree

This traditional breakfast dish has been popular since Victorian times. It has its origins in the Indian rice and lentil dish, Khichri, so it sometimes contains a little curry powder. Traditionally made from smoked haddock, kedgeree is even more delicious when made with cooked salmon.

⅔ cup long grain rice
salt
2 tablespoons lemon juice
⅔ cup heavy or sour
 cream
1 lb cooked salmon,
 flaked
pinch of cayenne
pinch of grated nutmeg
pepper
2 large eggs, hard-boiled

4 tablespoons unsalted
 butter
2 tablespoons chopped
 fresh parsley, to
 garnish
triangles of toast and
 parsley sprigs, to
 garnish

SERVES FOUR

Put the rice in a saucepan with 1⅓ cups of boiling, salted water and simmer for 15–20 minutes, until tender and the water has been absorbed. Remove from the heat and add the lemon juice, cream, salmon and seasonings.

Peel and chop the eggs and lightly mix into the rice. Turn the mixture into a buttered ovenproof dish, dot with the butter and bake in a preheated 350° oven for 30 minutes.

Stir in the chopped parsley. Arrange triangles of toast around the edge of the dish and garnish with sprigs of parsley.

Gloucester Cheese and Ale

This tasty recipe has been served as a farmhouse supper dish since the Middle Ages. It also used to be served in inns, with plenty of ale, when the poultry, meat or game were finished.

½ lb mild Cheddar,
 thinly sliced
1 teaspoon prepared
 English mustard
about ½ cup brown ale

4 thick slices of
 wholewheat bread
3 tablespoons brown ale,
 to serve

MAKES FOUR SLICES

Arrange the cheese slices in the bottom of a large shallow ovenproof dish and spread the mustard over the top.

Pour in enough brown ale just to cover the cheese. Cover with foil, then cook in a preheated 375° oven for about 10 minutes until the cheese has softened.

Meanwhile, toast the bread and remove the crusts. Gently warm 3 tablespoons brown ale. Sprinkle the warm ale over the toast and cover with melted cheese. Serve immediately.

FRICASSÉE OF EGGS (page 14) AND KEDGEREE (left)

Deviled Kidneys

This dish was very popular with the Edwardians especially for breakfast. Try to mix the sauce ingredients together in advance to allow their flavors to mingle and mature.

2 teaspoons
   Worcestershire sauce
1 tablespoon tomato paste
1 tablespoon lemon juice
1 tablespoon prepared
   English mustard
pinch of cayenne
salt and pepper

2 tablespoons unsalted
   butter
8 lamb's or calf's kidneys,
   skinned, halved, cores
   removed
1 tablespoon chopped
   fresh parsley, to
   garnish

SERVES FOUR

Blend the first six ingredients together in a bowl to make a sauce.

Melt the butter in a frying pan, add the halved kidneys and cook them over medium heat for about 3 minutes on each side.

Pour the sauce over the kidneys and quickly stir to coat them evenly. Serve immediately, sprinkled with chopped fresh parsley.

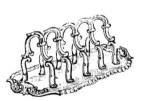

Mock Crab

Not all Victorian cooking was rich or elaborate, – this simple cheese dish would have been served at luncheon. Nowadays, it makes an ideal snack or supper dish.

1 hard-boiled egg yolk,
   sieved
1 tablespoon unsalted
   butter softened
1½ teaspoons prepared
   English mustard
⅛ teaspoon anchovy paste
pepper
1 cup grated Cheddar
   cheese

1 cup finely chopped and
   shredded cooked
   chicken breast
lettuce leaves, sliced
   tomato and cucumber
   and thinly sliced brown
   bread and butter, to
   serve

SERVES TWO OR THREE

Reserve a little of the egg yolk and mix the remainder with the butter, mustard, anchovy paste and pepper. Mix in the cheese with a fork so that it is evenly blended but as many shreds as possible of the cheese remain separate.

Mix in the chicken lightly, then taste and adjust the seasoning if necessary. Cover and leave in a cool place for at least 2 hours for the flavors to develop.

Serve on a small bed of lettuce, in crab shells if available, garnished with the reserved egg yolk and a little sliced tomato and cucumber. Serve thinly sliced brown bread and butter separately.

Fish and Shellfish Dishes

T IS only in comparatively recent times that the popularity and consumption of fish and shellfish have fallen, for not only does England have an extensive coastline with easy access to rich sea fishing grounds but it also has many rivers, streams and lakes that can supply an abundant quantity and diversity of first class freshwater fish to suit all tastes.

Until the sixteenth century and the Reformation the eating of fish on Fridays and other designated holy days was obligatory on religious grounds. After that, the State joined in and passed laws stating that fish only and not meat, should be eaten on Saturdays as well as Fridays – there was even an attempt to make Wednesday a fish-only day as well – to stimulate the fishing industry and in turn the shipbuilding industry and thus – with these industries flourishing – maintain England's prestige as a seafaring nation.

Because of its perishability and transport problems only those living near to the coast were ever able to taste fresh sea fish. The only experience inland dwellers had of such fish as cod and haddock were the dried or salted fairly non-perishable products. These were cheap, plentiful, and often of poor quality, and they therefore became a food of the poor. Freshwater fish, however, was widely available. Potting as a means of preservation was more expensive than drying or salting so was reserved for luxury foods, such as shrimp, to provide the more well-to-do living away from the coast with shellfish and the finer type of sea fish, such as sole.

With the introduction of the railways in the nineteenth century, the development of refrigeration techniques and the use of the first steam trawlers the movement of fresh fish around the country improved and for the first time many people were able to taste the true flavor of sea fish and shellfish.

Fish Cakes

Fish cakes have been a popular, quick dish since Victorian times. The type of cooked fish used can be varied according to what is available. More elaborate recipes also include a thick white sauce, which makes the cakes more like croquettes.

½ lb potatoes, cooked
4 tablespoons unsalted butter
12 oz salmon, cooked and flaked
1 tablespoon finely chopped fresh thyme or 1½ teaspoons dried
squeeze of lemon juice
salt and pepper

cayenne
1–2 eggs, beaten
3 tablespoons all-purpose flour
⅔ cup dry breadcrumbs
vegetable oil, for frying
watercress sprigs and lemon slices, to garnish

SERVES FOUR

Purée the potatoes or mash them well (there should be about 1 cup). Put into a saucepan, preferably non-stick, and heat gently, stirring, to dry them out completely. Beat in the butter.

Remove the pan from the heat and beat in the salmon, thyme, lemon juice and seasonings, and just enough egg to bind together. Leave to cool, then cover and chill.

Divide into four or eight portions, then, with floured hands, shape each portion into a flat cake. Coat in flour seasoned with salt and pepper, then the remaining egg, then the breadcrumbs.

Heat the oil in a frying pan, add the fish cakes and fry, turning once, until crisp and golden.

Drain on paper towels. Serve garnished with watercress and lemon slices.

Oyster Loaf

Now an expensive, luxury dish, this recipe dates from the time when oysters were cheap and plentiful. More economical modern versions can be made using mussels, or lightly cooked small scallops or clams, with a little fish stock in place of the oyster liquor.

1 miniature brioche or loaf of bread, or small roll
3 tablespoons melted unsalted butter
3 large oysters
2 tablespoons sour cream

2 tablespoons heavy cream
cayenne and white pepper
finely grated lemon rind and parsley sprig, to garnish

SERVES ONE

Remove the top knob from the brioche, or a slice from the top of the loaf or roll. Carefully scoop out all the inside, leaving just a wall of crust and taking care not to pierce the crust. Brush the crust shell, inside and out, with melted butter, place on a baking sheet and bake in a preheated 425° oven for 10 minutes.

Meanwhile, scrub the oysters then, holding each one in a cloth, flat side uppermost, pry open the shells at the hinge. Loosen the oysters, reserving their liquor. Add the liquor to the remaining melted butter in a saucepan, bring to a boil and boil for a few minutes to reduce the liquid.

Stir in the creams and boil until reduced to a sauce-like consistency, whisking with a small wire whisk. Season with white pepper and cayenne.

Put the oysters into the crust shell and spoon the sauce over them. Garnish with lemon rind and parsley.

Fish and Chips

Fish and chips eaten out of newspaper have been such a popular English dish for over a hundred years that they have almost become an institution. Serve sprinkled with salt and pepper and accompanied by vinegar.

1¼ lb potatoes, cut into sticks ⅛-inch square by 3 inches long	**Batter**
vegetable oil for deep frying	¾ cup self-rising flour
8 fillets of flounder or pieces of white fish such as haddock or cod	½ teaspoon baking powder
salt and pepper	1 teaspoon salt and white pepper
	⅔ cup milk
	SERVES FOUR

To make the batter, sift the flour and baking powder into a bowl and season. Make a well in the center, then gradually stir in the milk to make a smooth batter. Leave to stand for 30 minutes.

Rinse the potatoes in cold water, drain thoroughly, then dry well on paper towels or a dish towel.

Heat the oil in a deep fryer to 360°. Fill the basket about half-full with potatoes, then gently lower into the oil. Cook until the fries are a very light golden brown, shaking the basket occasionally to keep the fries from sticking together. Drain the fries well, then spread on a baking sheet lined with paper towels and place in a warm oven. Cook the remaining potatoes in the same way.

Keep the oil at 360°. Dry the fish well, coat in the batter, and fry until golden brown and crisp.

Remove with a slotted spoon and drain on paper towels.

Increase the temperature to 390°, add the fries and fry briefly to crisp them up. Drain on paper towels and season.

Herrings with Mustard Sauce

The piquancy of the sauce in this Cornish dish is a perfect foil for the richness of the herrings.

4 herrings, cleaned, heads removed	2 tablespoons sour cream
salt and pepper	salt and white pepper
lemon juice, to taste	a selection of large capers, cocktail onions and gherkins cut into fan shapes, to serve
Sauce	
2 teaspoons mustard powder	
2 egg yolks	SERVES FOUR
4 tablespoons unsalted butter, diced	

Season the herrings inside and out with salt, pepper and lemon juice. Broil for 3–5 minutes on each side.

Meanwhile, prepare the sauce. Blend the mustard with the egg yolks in a bowl, then place over a saucepan of hot water and whisk until creamy.

Gradually whisk in the butter until it has all been incorporated and the sauce is thick. Remove from the heat and whisk in the cream. Season.

Place the herrings on warmed serving plates, spoon the sauce to one side of the fish. Serve with a selection of large capers, cocktail onions and gherkins cut into fan shapes.

Fish Pies

Recipes for fish pies abound as they are a useful way of using up cooked fish. Any fish can be used, although cod and haddock feature most frequently. The covering can be potato, basic pie, flaky or puff pastry, or, as in this more unusual recipe, choux pastry.

2 tablespoons unsalted
  butter
1 shallot, finely chopped
white part of 1 long, thin
  leek, finely sliced
½ cup diced mushrooms
2 tablespoons all-purpose
  flour
1¼ cups milk
1 lb cooked white fish,
  flaked
2 oz peeled shrimp
2 oz shelled mussels
salt and pepper

cayenne
lemon juice, to taste

Topping
⅔ cup all-purpose flour
4 tablespoons unsalted
  butter, diced
¾ cup water
2 eggs, beaten
1 teaspoon mixed dried
  herbs
salt and pepper

SERVES SIX

Melt the butter, add the shallot and leek and cook over a medium heat, stirring occasionally, until softened. Stir in the mushrooms and cook the vegetables for 2–3 minutes.

Stir in the flour and cook for 2 minutes. Gradually stir in the milk, then bring to a boil, stirring, and simmer for 5 minutes, stirring occasionally. Remove from the heat and stir in the fish, shrimp, mussels, seasonings and lemon juice.

Spoon the mixture into six buttered 3½-inch ovenproof dishes.

To make the choux paste for the topping, sift the flour onto a sheet of wax paper. Put the butter and water into a saucepan and heat until the butter has melted, then bring to the boil and immediately pour in all the flour. Remove the pan from the heat and beat until the dough is smooth and leaves the sides of the pan. Cool slightly, then gradually beat in the eggs, beating well after each addition. Add the seasonings and mixed dried herbs.

Spoon the paste into a pastry bag and pipe small bun shapes over the top of each of the dishes. Bake in a preheated 425° oven for about 20 minutes, then reduce the temperature to 375° and continue baking until the choux pastry topping is cooked in the center.

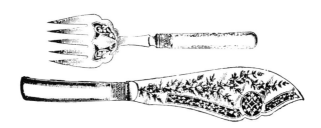

Fish Pudding

This light, moist pudding can be made with any type of cooked fish or combination of fish or shellfish. Use a melon baller to make the cucumber balls.

1¼ cups milk or heavy cream
2 bay leaves
½ cup fresh breadcrumbs
3 egg yolks, beaten
12 oz fish, cooked and flaked
4 oz peeled shrimp, chopped
½ teaspoon anchovy paste
3 tablespoons snipped chives

salt and pepper
lemon juice, to taste
shrimp, chervil or parsley sprigs and steamed cucumber balls, to garnish

SERVES FOUR

Put the milk or cream and the bay leaves in a small saucepan and heat gently to simmering point. Pour over the breadcrumbs in a bowl and leave to soak for 10 minutes.

Remove the bay leaves, then beat in the egg yolks. Stir in the fish, shrimp, anchovy paste and chives. Season with a very little salt, pepper and lemon juice. Pour into a buttered 1-quart steaming mold or deep pan. Cover with wax paper, stand in a deep baking pan and add enough boiling water to come halfway up the sides of the mold. Cook in a preheated 350° oven for about 1 hour 10 minutes until just set.

Remove the mold from the heat and leave to stand for about 2 minutes before unmolding. Garnish with shrimp, chervil sprigs and steamed cucumber balls.

Water-Souchy

The name of this light fish stew (which can also be spelled water sootje) is a corruption of the Belgian waterzootje, and it reflects the strong links that existed between England and the Low Countries from Tudor times. Water-souchy is a simple fish stew that depends on the quality and freshness of the fish, the flavor of the stock and the delicacy of the cooking for success. Any combination of fish can be used, grand or humble, to suit the pocket or occasion.

4 tablespoons unsalted butter
1 quart good fish stock
white part of 1 thin leek, chopped
1 celery stalk, chopped
1 small carrot, finely chopped
bouquet garni of 1 bay leaf, 3 chervil sprigs and 2 parsley sprigs

2 lb mixed fish, eg carp, perch, trout, mackerel, mullet, prepared and cut into 1 inch pieces
sea salt and white pepper
finely chopped fresh parsley, to garnish

SERVES FOUR

Melt the butter in a saucepan, add 3 tablespoons of the stock and the vegetables. Cover and cook over a low heat, shaking the saucepan occasionally, for 5–7 minutes until the carrot is almost tender.

Add the remaining stock and the bouquet garni and bring to a boil. Reduce the heat so the liquid just simmers and add the fish. Cook with the liquid barely moving for about 5 minutes until the fish is just tender. Season and remove the bouquet garni.

Serve sprinkled with plenty of chopped parsley.

Dressed Crab

With its elegant simplicity, this is one of the best ways of serving top class crabs like those caught in the West Country, on the east coast of England or in California or Delaware.

1 uncooked crab, about
   2 lb
3 parsley stems
1 bay leaf
small sprig of thyme
salt and 5 white
   peppercorns, crushed
1 tablespoon white wine
   vinegar
2 tablespoons fresh
   brown breadcrumbs
2 teaspoons lemon juice
white pepper

1 tablespoon mayonnaise
   (optional)
1 egg, hard-boiled
2 teaspoons finely
   chopped fresh parsley
paprika
lettuce leaves, hard-
   boiled egg slices
   (optional) and
   cucumber twists, to
   garnish

SERVES FOUR

Place the crab in a large saucepan with the herbs, salt, peppercorns and vinegar. Cover with cold water and bring very slowly to a boil, then cover and simmer for 20 minutes. Cool in the water.

Place the crab on its back on a board with the tail flap towards you. Twist off the legs and claws close to the body, then remove the body. Discard the grayish-white gills attached to the body and the stomach bag attached to the back shell, plus any greenish matter from the shell.

Carefully scrape the brown meat from the shell into a bowl using the handle of a teaspoon to get right under the shell. Scrape the pinkish curd into the bowl. Crack the claws and legs using a hammer or heavy weight and remove as much white meat as possible. Place in a separate bowl.

Tap around the shell to the natural dark line to neaten it, then scrub the shell, dry it well and rub lightly with oil to make it shine.

Mix the breadcrumbs, 1 teaspoon of the lemon juice and seasoning into the brown meat, then pack neatly into the center of the shell, leaving room on either side for the white meat.

Season the white meat and stir in the remaining lemon juice and the mayonnaise, if using. Arrange the white meat in the sides of the shell.

Separate the yolk and white of the egg. Chop the white finely and sieve the yolk. Sprinkle a straight line of egg yolk along the lines where the white meat meets the brown. Sprinkle a row of parsley next to the two rows of yolk then a row of egg white next to the parsley rows. Sprinkle paprika in diagonal lines over the white meat to make a diamond pattern.

Place the shell on a small bed of shredded lettuce and garnish the lettuce with halved hard-boiled egg slices, if liked, and cucumber twists.

DRESSED CRAB (above)

Soles in Coffins

A delicious Victorian luncheon dish with a tongue-in-cheek play on the word sole (soul) in the title. It is not as complicated as it may at first seem as it is no more than a series of simple steps that can be prepared separately.

4 large potatoes	1¼ cups milk
8 small sole fillets, skinned	pinch of ground mace
salt and white pepper	1 cup sliced mushrooms
2 shallots, finely chopped	4 oz peeled shrimp
scant 1 cup dry white wine	parsley sprigs or peas, to garnish
10 tablespoons unsalted butter, diced	baked small tomatoes, to serve
6 tablespoons all-purpose flour	SERVES FOUR

Bake the potatoes in a preheated 400° oven for about 1½ hours until soft.

Season the fillets, then roll them up skinned side inwards. Scatter the shallots over the bottom of a heavy frying pan or shallow flameproof casserole that is just large enough to hold the fish. Place the rolls on the shallots, pour the wine over, cover with wax paper and poach for 4–5 minutes until they just flake – it is important not to overcook them. Carefully remove the rolls from the pan.

Melt 4 tablespoons of the butter in a saucepan, stir in the flour and cook gently for 2 minutes, stirring. Remove from the heat and gradually stir in 1 cup of the milk, then strain in the fish cooking liquid. Bring to a boil, stirring, then simmer for 2 minutes. Add the mace and seasoning and remove from the heat.

Cut a slice from each potato then, using a teaspoon, carefully scoop out the center and reserve.

Melt 2 tablespoons of the remaining butter, add the mushrooms and cook for 2 minutes. Stir in the shrimp and cook for 1 minute, stirring occasionally. Divide the sauce between the potatoes. Place two rolls of sole in each potato, add the mushrooms and shrimp and replace the slices of potato.

Place the potatoes on a baking sheet and bake in a 350° oven for 10 minutes. Meanwhile, mash the reserved potato flesh with the remaining butter and milk. Season well.

Arrange the mashed potato around the edge of a large warmed serving plate and garnish with parsley or peas. Place the baked potatoes in the center. Serve with baked small tomatoes.

Salmon with Fennel Sauce

In the past, salmon was plentiful in English and American rivers. Over-fishing and pollution decreased numbers but now, as a result of controlled fishing and cleaner waters, wild salmon is beginning to be seen once again in the shops.

4 salmon steaks, about
  6 oz each
2 shallots, chopped
1 fennel bulb, quartered
1 bay leaf
2 parsley sprigs, crushed
⅔ cup dry white wine
2 egg yolks

8 tablespoons (1 stick)
  unsalted butter,
  softened
salt and white pepper
lemon juice, to taste
fennel sprigs, to garnish

SERVES FOUR

Place the salmon steaks in a shallow ovenproof dish. Scatter the shallots, fennel, bay leaf and parsley over the top. Pour in the wine, cover tightly and bake in a preheated 350° oven for 15 minutes.

Strain off ½ cup of the cooking liquid. Turn off the oven, recover the salmon and keep warm.

Boil the strained liquid until reduced to 1 tablespoon. Blend the egg yolks together in a bowl, then stir in the reduced liquid and work in half the butter. Place the bowl over a saucepan of hot water and whisk with a balloon whisk until the butter has melted. Gradually whisk in the remaining butter, whisking well after each addition. Remove from heat.

Chop enough of the fennel to yield 2 teaspoons, then add to the sauce with the seasoning, adding a little lemon juice, if necessary.

Transfer the salmon to a warmed plate. Spoon over the fennel sauce and garnish with fennel sprigs.

Mackerel with Gooseberry Sauce

This gooseberry sauce should be sharp to complement the richness of the mackerel. Unless the fruit is particularly green and tart, sugar is unnecessary.

1 tablespoon unsalted
  butter
½ lb gooseberries, ends
  trimmed
4 mackerel, cleaned,
  heads removed

salt and pepper
lemon juice, to taste
1 egg beaten

SERVES FOUR

Melt the butter in a saucepan and add the gooseberries. Cover tightly and cook over a low heat, shaking the pan occasionally, until the gooseberries are tender.

Meanwhile, season the mackerel inside and out with salt, plenty of black pepper and lemon juice. Make two or three slashes with the point of a sharp knife in the skin on each side of the fish, then broil for 15–20 minutes, depending on size, turning once.

Purée the gooseberries in a blender or food processor or press through a sieve. Pour the purée into a clean pan, beat in the egg, then reheat gently, stirring. Season with salt and pepper. Place the mackerel on warmed serving plates and spoon the sauce beside the fish.

Cornish Buttered Lobster

The quality of Cornish lobsters has been famed for many years and for a magnificent dish like this such quality is essential.

2 lobsters, about 1½ lb each, split into halves	3 tablespoons heavy cream
lemon juice	salt and pepper
8 tablespoons (1 stick) unsalted butter	pinch of cayenne
¼ cup fresh white breadcrumbs	cucumber twists, lemon slices and dill sprigs, to garnish
3 tablespoons brandy	
	SERVES FOUR

Discard the stomach, the dark vein that runs through the body, and the spongy gills from each lobster. Remove the tail meat. Crack open the claws and remove the meat. Scrape the meat from the legs with a skewer. Cut the meat into chunks and sprinkle with lemon juice. Remove and reserve the coral (roe), if present. Remove and reserve the soft pink flesh and liver separately.

Scrub the shells and place in a low oven to warm. Melt 4 tablespoons of the butter in a frying pan, add the breadcrumbs and cook until browned and crisp.

Meanwhile, melt the remaining butter in a saucepan, add the lobster meat and stir gently until heated through.

Warm the brandy in a ladle, ignite and pour, still flaming, over the lobster. When the flames have subsided, transfer the lobster to the warmed shells using a slotted spoon and keep warm in a low oven.

Pound the liver and pink flesh. Stir into the cooking juices with the cream, a little salt and cayenne and plenty of black pepper. Boil briefly until thickened, then spoon over the lobster. Sprinkle the fried breadcrumbs over the top. Quickly garnish with the reserved coral, if available, cucumber twists, lemon slices and dill sprigs.

Jugged Kippers

Kippers are herrings that have been split down the back and immersed for a short while in a very concentrated brine solution that gives the characteristic glossy sheen after drying and 4–6 hours light smoking. Originally, kippers were a pale, silvery-gold color, but the practice of adding a dye to turn them a mahogany color is now commonplace. For jugged kippers, try to find undyed kippers – then this simple method will show just how good kippers can be.

4 kippers	thin slices of brown bread, to serve
lemon wedges, parsley sprigs and a pat of unsalted butter (optional), to garnish	
	SERVES FOUR

Stand the kippers tail end up in a deep stoneware jar. Pour boiling water over the fish, but not the tails. Cover with a cloth and leave for 5 minutes.

Pour the water from the jug, then carefully remove the kippers, but not by their tails or they may break.

Serve on warmed plates with lemon wedges, parsley sprigs and a pat of unsalted butter, if wished. Serve the jugged kippers with thin slices of brown bread.

SOLE "STEWED" IN CREAM (page 31)

Arundel Mullet

Mullet, especially the finer-fleshed red mullet, has been a favorite fish in England for hundreds of years although, like many varieties, it almost disappeared in the 1940s. Now it is making a comeback and is becoming more readily available. In this recipe, which dates from the seventeenth century, the combination of red and white wine produces a style that is more like the old "clairet" than present day claret (Bordeaux wine).

4 mullet	3 lemon slices, rind and
⅔ cup dry white wine	pith removed
⅔ cup light, fruity red	3 tablespoons unsalted
wine	butter, diced
3 anchovy fillets	small thyme sprigs and
pinch of freshly grated	snipped chives, to
nutmeg	garnish
sprig of thyme	
1 bay leaf	SERVES FOUR
salt and white pepper	

Make three slashes with the point of a sharp knife in the skin on either side of each fish. Arrange them in a single layer in a large frying pan that will just hold them comfortably, then add the white and red wines, anchovy fillets, nutmeg and the thyme sprig and bay leaf.

Cover with wax paper and poach gently for about 20–25 minutes until the flesh is almost tender. Carefully lift the mullet from the liquid, using a slotted spatula, and set them aside on a warmed plate. Boil the fish cooking liquid, uncovered, until it is reduced by half.

Remove the herbs, add the seasoning and lemon slices, then return the fish to the pan and cook gently for a further 5 minutes. Transfer the fish to warmed plates. Gradually whisk the butter into the sauce. Garnish, and serve the fish with the sauce spooned around it.

Haddock and Parsley Sauce

A classic English dish that is at its best when made with really fresh haddock.

4 haddock fillets, about	3 tablespoons finely
6 oz each	chopped fresh parsley
salt and pepper	lemon juice, to taste
½ cup milk	diced tomato flesh and
¾ cup heavy cream	flat-leaved parsley, to
¾ cup fish stock	garnish
2 small egg yolks	
2 tablespoons unsalted	SERVES FOUR
butter, diced	

Place the haddock in a shallow saucepan, season well, add the milk and cream and bring slowly to simmering point. Cover and poach for 5 minutes.

Meanwhile, put the stock in a saucepan and boil until reduced to 2 tablespoons.

Transfer the fish to a warmed shallow dish, cover and keep warm. Stir a little of the cooking liquid into the reduced stock, then blend into the egg yolks. Bring the remaining liquid to a boil, then gradually blend into the egg yolks. Return to the rinsed out pan and heat gently, stirring, until thickened. Do not allow to boil. Stir in the butter and the parsley.

Remove from the heat, season and add a little lemon juice if necessary. Divide between four warmed plates and place the fish beside the sauce. Garnish with diced tomato and flat-leaved parsley.

Sole "Stewed" in Cream

The old name for this dish should not be taken too literally – the liquid should barely bubble and the fish only be cooked briefly. With the attractive presentation, it would have been served as a fish course at an elegant luncheon.

4 sole fillets, skinned and cut in half lengthwise	*Garnish*
2 tablespoons unsalted butter	lobster or salmon roe
1 tablespoon finely chopped shallot	cooked crayfish or shrimp
1¼ cups fish stock	puff pastry fleurons or croûtes of bread
blade of mace	parsley sprigs
1 cup heavy cream	lemon twists
salt and white pepper	
	SERVES FOUR

Tie each strip of sole into a loose knot in the center. Melt half the butter in a large frying pan, add the shallot, cover and cook, shaking the pan occasionally, until softened. Stir in the stock and mace and boil rapidly until reduced to ¼ cup. Remove the mace.

Stir in half the cream and bring to a boil. Lower the heat, season lightly and gently lower the fish into the pan. Spoon cream over the fish. Cover with buttered wax paper and poach gently for about 3 minutes until the fish just flakes.

Carefully transfer the fish to a warmed plate using a slotted spatula, cover and keep warm. Boil the cooking liquid until slightly thickened. Stir in the remaining butter and adjust the seasoning, if necessary.

Spoon the sauce over four warmed plates. Arrange the fish on top and garnish attractively with lobster or salmon roe, crayfish or sprimp, puff pastry fleurons or croûtes of bread, parsley and lemon twists.

Meat Dishes

THE ENGLISH have always enjoyed eating meat and for a long time thought that the amount of meat in the diet indicated the level of success and prosperity. It was only the better-off who could afford to have ample supplies and, indeed, they would tend to eat meat, usually roasted, almost to the exclusion of all else, except game.

The less wealthy could only afford the cheaper cuts that needed slow, moist cooking to make them tender. The meat was frequently stretched with vegetables and cereals, thus developing the tasty casseroles, stews, puddings and pies that are a strong feature in English cooking.

Only the very rich and influential could afford fresh meat during the winter months. Most households had to make do with the salted, cured and potted meats that were traditionally prepared in the autumn when the breeding stock was slaughtered.

Nowadays, it is not necessary to kill off livestock with the approach of winter and modern methods of preservation and refrigeration have done away with the necessity for using salt to keep meat palatable. However, ham and bacon are still prepared in large quantities simply because they are part of the English way of eating. Sausages were a by-product of the autumnal slaughter but they, too, exist now because of their popularity not just out of necessity.

Melton Mowbray Pork Pie

*Raised pork pies are made all over England but
more especially in the hunting shire counties.
The distinguishing feature of a Melton Mowbray
pie is the inclusion of a small amount of
anchovy flavoring.*

2 lb lean boneless pork,
  cut into ¼-inch dice
3 bacon slices, finely
  diced
1 teaspoon finely chopped
  fresh sage or
  ½ teaspoon dried
1 teaspoon finely chopped
  fresh thyme or
  ½ teaspoon dried
¼ teaspoon anchovy paste
½ teaspoon ground mace
½ teaspoon ground
  allspice
salt and pepper

2 cups concentrated beef
  stock
beaten egg, for glazing

Hot Water Crust Pastry
3¼ cups all-purpose flour
pinch of salt
1 egg yolk
6 oz (¾ cup) lard, diced
½–¾ cup mixed milk and
  water

SERVES SIX TO EIGHT

To make the pastry, warm a mixing bowl and sift
the flour and salt into it. Make a well in the center
and add the egg yolk.

Gently heat the lard in the milk and water until it
has melted then bring the liquid rapidly to a boil.
Pour immediately into the well in the flour and draw
the ingredients together with a wooden spoon to
form a soft, pliable but not sticky ball of dough.

Transfer to a lightly floured surface and knead
until it is smooth and a slight resistance develops.
Cover the dough with plastic wrap and leave to rest
in a warm place for 20–30 minutes.

Mix together the pork, bacon, sage, thyme,
anchovy paste, spices, and a little salt and pepper.
Moisten with 3 tablespoons of the stock.

Roll out two-thirds of the pastry on a lightly
floured surface and mold around a 1-quart floured
straight-sided jar, or line a raised pie mold or hinged
pâté mold. If using a jar, leave the pastry to set on a
baking sheet, then gently ease out the jar.

Pack the meat mixture into the pastry. Roll out the
remaining pastry to make a lid for the pie. Press the
edges together tightly to seal them. Scallop the
edges and make two small holes at opposite sides or
ends of the lid and insert a funnel of foil in each. Tie
a double thickness of buttered parchment paper
around the outside of the pie if formed using a jar.
Brush the top with beaten egg. Place on a baking
sheet if using a mold.

Bake in a preheated 400° oven for 20 minutes,
then reduce the temperature to 350° and cook for a
further 2¼ hours. Remove the mold or parchment
paper, brush the sides and top with egg and return
to the oven for 10–15 minutes until well browned.

Remove the pie from the oven and leave until
almost cold. Heat the stock to the consistency of egg
white. Remove the foil funnel and pour in the stock
through a funnel. Leave the pie in a cool place
overnight.

Steak, Kidney and Oyster Pudding

The meat for this dish can be cooked from raw in the pastry case, but because a longer steaming time is needed the pastry tends to become a little soggy and heavy. In this recipe the meat is cooked beforehand, and the flavor of the filling is improved by the overnight standing; surplus fat can also be removed. The addition of oysters dates from the days of Mrs. Beeton, when they were cheap. They can be replaced by additional mushrooms if wished.

2 tablespoons beef drippings or bacon fat
1 onion, chopped
1½ lb beef for stew, trimmed and cut into 1-inch cubes
2 tablespoons all-purpose flour
5 oz lamb or beef kidney, trimmed and cut into 1-inch cubes
4 oz mushrooms
2 cups brown stock, preferably veal, or half stock and half brown ale or dark beer
bouquet garni of 1 bay leaf, 6 parsley sprigs, sprig of thyme
1 dozen oysters (optional)

Crust
1⅔ cups self-rising flour
1 teaspoon baking powder
salt and pepper
1 teaspoon finely grated lemon rind
1 tablespoon finely chopped fresh parsley
⅓ cup shredded suet
4 tablespoons hard unsalted butter, finely diced
1 egg, beaten

SERVES FOUR

The day before the pudding is required, melt half the drippings in a frying pan, add the onion and cook for 2–3 minutes.

Coat the beef in flour seasoned with salt and pepper, then add to the pan and fry, stirring occasionally, until lightly browned. Transfer to a casserole.

Coat the kidney in seasoned flour, stir into the pan and cook for 2–3 minutes. Add to the casserole.

Melt the remaining drippings and cook the mushrooms for 2–3 minutes. Add to the casserole. Stir in the stock, and brown ale if using, into the pan, dislodging the sediment, and bring to a boil. Add the bouquet garni and seasoning and pour over the meat. Stir, then cover tightly and cook in a preheated 350° oven for 1½–2 hours. Leave, covered, in a cool place overnight.

The day of eating, stir the flour, baking powder, seasoning, lemon rind and parsley together. Stir in the suet and butter, then add the egg and sufficient water to give a soft, pliable but not sticky dough.

Knead lightly, then on a lightly floured surface, roll out to a 10-inch round. Cut out one-quarter of the dough in a fan shape to within 1 inch of the center.

Remove the bouquet garni and the fat from the surface of the meat. If there is an excessive amount of liquid, pour it off and boil it until reduced. (This is not so important if oysters are not usd.)

Scrub the oysters then, holding each one in a cloth, flat side uppermost, pry open the shells at the hinge. Loosen the oysters and add them, with their liquor, to the meat. Check the seasoning.

Line a 3½-cup steaming mold with three-quarters of the dough and fill with the meat and oyster mixture. Roll out the remaining piece of dough to a round 1 inch larger than the top of the mold. Dampen the exposed edge of the dough lining the mold. Lift the round of dough on top of the meat and oyster filling and press the dough edges together to seal.

Cover with a circle of wax paper, then a piece of foil pleated across the center and tie in place with string.

Put the mold in a large saucepan with enough boiling water to come halfway up the sides of the mold. Cover and steam for 1½–2 hours, replenishing with boiling water if necessary. Serve the pudding in the mold with a white napkin or cloth tied around it.

Leg of Lamb with Crabmeat Stuffing

This is based on an early nineteenth century recipe, the flavors of which combine extremely well without overpowering each other. The original recipe calls for a crab or lobster sauce to be served under the leg but a more practical herb-flavored English butter sauce works as well, if not better. The dill complements both lamb and crab.

4 lb leg of lamb, boned
salt and pepper
½ lb crabmeat
½ cup fresh breadcrumbs
finely grated rind of
    1 lemon
freshly grated nutmeg
pinch of cayenne
1 egg yolk
1 celery stalk, finely
    chopped
white part of 1 thin leek,
    finely chopped
6 tablespoons dry white
    wine

Sauce
½ lb (2 sticks) unsalted
    butter, diced
2½ tablespoons all-
    purpose flour
⅔ cup water
about 1½ tablespoons
    finely chopped fresh
    dill or 2 teaspoons
    dried
lemon juice, to taste
salt and white pepper

SERVES FOUR TO SIX

Season the lamb inside and out. Mix the crabmeat, breadcrumbs, lemon rind, nutmeg, cayenne and seasoning together. Bind lightly with egg yolk. Fill the cavity in the leg with the mixture and sew it up.

Place the celery and leek in a casserole. Season and place the lamb on top. Pour the wine over, cover and cook in a preheated 350° oven for about 1½ hours until the lamb is almost tender.

Transfer the lamb to a rack placed in a roasting pan and return it to the oven for about 20 minutes to brown the outside.

Meanwhile, make the sauce. Melt one-third of the butter. Blend the flour with the water and whisk into the melted butter using a balloon whisk. Heat to simmering point then leave over a low heat for about 20 minutes, stirring occasionally.

Gradually whisk in the remaining butter, making sure each piece is fully incorporated before adding the next. Add the dill and lemon juice to taste and season with salt and pepper.

While the sauce is cooking over a low heat, leave the lamb in a warm place for about 15 minutes.

Serve the lamb, carved into slices, accompanied by the dill and butter sauce.

Lamb Cutlets Reform

*This dish was created by Alexis Soyer when he was chef at the Reform Club in Pall Mall. He poured the classic French sauce, **poivrade**, over a garnish of hard-boiled egg white, mushrooms, truffles, tongue and gherkins and served ham and breaded mutton or lamb on the side accompanied by red currant jelly.*

12–18 lamb rib chops, depending on size
1 egg, beaten
about 1½ cups fresh white breadcrumbs
2 tablespoons very finely chopped cooked ham
4 tablespoons unsalted butter

Sauce
2 tablespoons vegetable oil
2 large onions, chopped
2 carrots, chopped
1 celery stalk, chopped
2 tablespoons all-purpose flour
½ cup red wine vinegar
2 cups dry white wine
4 juniper berries, lightly crushed

bouquet garni of 6 parsley sprigs, 1 bay leaf and a sprig of thyme
2 quarts brown stock, preferably veal
10 black peppercorns, lightly crushed and tied in cheesecloth
salt

Garnish
white of 2 hard-boiled eggs
2 mushroom caps
1 oz cooked tongue
1 gherkin
¾ oz truffle (optional)
red currant jelly, to serve

SERVES FOUR TO SIX

First make the sauce: heat the oil in a large saucepan, add the vegetables and cook, stirring occasionally, until golden brown.

Sprinkle the flour over and cook gently, stirring frequently, until a rich golden brown. Stir in the vinegar and half the wine, dislodging any sediment, and cook gently until the liquid is reduced to a syrupy consistency.

Stir in the remaining wine, the juniper berries, bouquet garni and stock. Simmer gently, removing any scum occasionally, for about 3 hours until the sauce is well reduced.

Pass the sauce through a conical strainer or fine sieve, pressing down on the vegetables, then strain through cheesecloth into a clean saucepan. Add the peppercorns and simmer for about 10 minutes. Adjust the seasoning and either boil to reduce to about 2½ cups or add extra stock if necessary. Remove the peppercorns.

Coat the lamb chops in egg, allowing the excess to drain off. Mix the breadcrumbs and ham together on a flat plate. Coat the lamb chops evenly and lightly in the breadcrumb and ham mixture, pressing it well into the surface.

Melt three-quarters of the butter in a large frying pan and cook the lamb for 3–4 minutes on each side, depending upon their thickness. Fry them in batches if necessary so they are not crowded in the pan and add extra butter as necessary.

Cut the garnish ingredients into fine strips, mix together and arrange on a warmed large serving platter, leaving plenty of space for the lamb. Carefully pour the sauce over the garnish and arrange the lamb chops next to it. Serve the chops with red currant jelly.

LAMB CUTLETS REFORM (above)

Boiled Beef and Carrots

A classic Cockney way of cooking beef that had been preserved for the winter months by salting. Check whether the meat is well-cured (thus excessively salty) and needs soaking.

3½ lb lean corned beef
  brisket
bouquet garni of 1 bay
  leaf, 6 parsley sprigs,
  small sprig of
  rosemary,
  sprig of thyme
6 black peppercorns,
  lightly crushed
2 small onions, quartered
  and a clove stuck in
  each quarter

1 carrot, quartered
2 small turnips, quartered
2 celery stalks, chopped
1 leek, chopped
12 small carrots
peas and mashed potatoes
  or dumplings, to serve

SERVES FOUR TO SIX

Place the beef in a large saucepan, add just enough water to cover and bring slowly to a boil. Remove the scum from the surface, add the bouquet garni, peppercorns, onion, carrot quarters, turnip, celery and leek. Lower the heat and simmer very gently for about 2 hours. Add the small carrots and simmer gently for a further 30–40 minutes or until the carrots are tender.

Carefully transfer the beef and small carrots to a warmed serving plate and keep warm. Strain the cooking liquid and remove the fat from the surface. Boil the liquid to reduce slightly then pour into a warmed sauceboat.

Serve the beef surrounded by the carrots, accompanied by peas and mashed potatoes or dumplings, with the sauce passed separately.

Beef Olives

The actual origin of the name of this very English of dishes is a little uncertain – it is most likely that it is so called because the shape resembles olives. It has been popular from the early 1800s and this is one of the most tasty versions.

⅓ cup chopped bacon
1 small onion, chopped
2 teaspoons finely
  chopped fresh parsley
2 cups fresh breadcrumbs
¼ cup shredded suet
¼ teaspoon mixed dried
  herbs
1 lemon
1 small egg, beaten
salt and pepper
about 2 lb boneless top
  round of beef, cut into
  8 thin slices
about 1 tablespoon
  prepared English
  mustard
2 bacon slices, chopped
2 shallots, chopped

1 carrot, chopped
1 very small turnip,
  chopped
1¼ cups brown stock,
  preferably veal
⅔ cup red wine
¼ cup Marsala
1 bay leaf
parsley sprigs, to garnish
baby carrots, baby
  turnips and whole
  shallots, to serve

SERVES FOUR

Mix the first six ingredients together, add the grated rind of half the lemon and 1 teaspoon of the juice. Bind together with the egg, then season.

Flatten each slice of beef between two sheets of damp wax paper, then spread sparingly with mustard. Divide the stuffing between the slices, fold the sides over and roll up into neat parcels. Secure with fine string.

Heat the slices of bacon gently in a shallow flameproof casserole until the fat runs, then remove the bacon with a slotted spoon. Place the beef rolls in the casserole and fry over medium heat until lightly browned. Remove with a slotted spoon.

Add the shallots, carrot and turnip and fry until the shallots are beginning to soften. Stir in the stock, wine and Marsala, and bring to a boil. Return the bacon and beef rolls to the casserole, add the bay leaf and season lightly. Cover with foil and the lid and cook in a preheated 325° oven for about 1½ hours.

Transfer the beef rolls to a warmed serving plate, remove the bay leaf from the liquid and purée the liquid. Bring to a boil and boil for a few minutes to thicken it slightly. Adjust the seasoning and pour over the beef.

Garnish with parsley sprigs and serve surrounded by baby carrots, baby turnips and whole shallots.

Pomes Dorryle

The modern name for this dish, which is basically a type of pork meatball, would be Glazed or Gilded Apples. In the medieval recipe on which this version is based, the gilding took the form of a thick paste of flour, honey and saffron, a combination which is a little expensive and not quite to today's tastes.

1 lb ground lean pork	about ¼ cup fresh white
1 tablespoon finely	breadcrumbs
chopped fresh	white pepper
marjoram or	vegetable oil for deep
1½ teaspoons dried	frying
3 sage leaves, finely	fried apple rings or apple
chopped	sauce and watercress,
½ teaspoon ground mace	to serve
salt and pepper	
3 eggs, beaten	SERVES FOUR

Mix the pork, herbs, mace and salt and pepper together, then bind with two thirds of the beaten egg. Form the mixture into 12 small balls, place on a rack in a roasting pan and bake in a preheated 350° oven for about 20 minutes. Leave to cool.

Mix the breadcrumbs with salt and white pepper. Coat the pork balls in the remaining egg, allowing the excess to drain off, then toss in the breadcrumbs until coated.

Heat the oil in a deep fryer to 350°. Add the pork balls and fry for 3–4 minutes until crisp and golden. Drain on paper towels, then serve immediately with fried apple rings or apple sauce and watercress.

Veal Collops

A collop or escalope is a thick slice of boned meat cut across the grain which is then flattened before cooking. It can be beef, venison, lamb or, as in this recipe, veal.

4 veal cutlets or scallops, about 4 oz each, cut in half	2 teaspoons all-purpose flour
5 tablespoons unsalted butter	salt and pepper
	pinch of ground mace
1 small onion, chopped	
¾ cup dry white wine	*Garnish*
1¼ cups veal stock	crisp bacon rolls
1–2 drops tabasco	button mushroom caps
mushroom	lemon twists
about 1 tablespoon lemon juice	parsley sprigs
	SERVES FOUR

Flatten each veal cutlet between two sheets of damp wax paper.

Melt 4 tablespoons butter in a frying pan, add the veal and cook for about 2 minutes on each side. Transfer to a warmed plate and keep warm.

Add the onion to the pan and cook for about 3 minutes, stirring frequently, until softened but not browned. Stir in the wine and boil until almost evaporated. Stir in the stock, tabasco and lemon juice, bring to a boil and simmer until reduced to 1 cup.

Work the flour into the remaining butter, then gradually whisk into the stock to thicken it slightly. Season with salt, pepper and mace, taste and add more ketchup and lemon juice if necessary.

Arrange the veal slices, overlapping each other, on a warmed oval meat platter. Spoon some of the sauce down the center of the collops and garnish with bacon rolls, mushroom caps, lemon twists and parsley sprigs. Serve the remaining sauce separately.

Beef Hare

A tougher cut of beef when cooked slowly and spiced like this, is beautifully tender and has a flavor like hare.

2 lb beef chuck, cut into strips about 3×1 inch	1 onion, cut into quarters and each piece stuck with 2 cloves
flour seasoned with salt, pepper and plenty of freshly grated nutmeg	1 small young parsnip, shredded
1 teaspoon celery seeds	⅔ cup red wine
	SERVES FOUR

Toss the meat in the seasoned flour, then pack into a deep 1-quart earthenware pot, scattering celery seeds in between the layers.

Arrange the onion and parsnip on top, pour in the wine, cover tightly and leave for about 2 hours.

Place in a preheated 425° oven and immediately reduce the temperature to 325°. Cook for 2¼ hours or until the beef is tender.

VEAL COLLOPS (above)

Spiced Beef

Spiced beef is traditional Christmas fare in Leicestershire, and parts of Yorkshire. It is ideal for a buffet at any time of the year, for picnics or packed meals. Once cooked it can be kept, well-wrapped, in the refrigerator for 1–2 weeks.

4 lb lean, boned top round beef roast	½ cup dark brown sugar
⅓ cup sea or kosher salt	1½ teaspoons saltpeter
1 tablespoon crushed juniper berries	⅔ cup red wine
1 tablespoon cloves	*To serve*
1 tablespoon crushed black peppercorns	horseradish sauce
	beets
1 tablespoon whole allspice	thinly sliced brown bread and butter or crusty bread
1 blade of mace	
1 bay leaf	pickled onions and other pickles
1 teaspoon chopped fresh thyme or ½ teaspoon dried	
	SERVES SIX TO EIGHT

Rub all the surfaces of the beef with the salt, roll the meat up and place it in an earthenware pot. Cover and leave in a cool place overnight.

Crush the spices and herbs together, then crush with the sugar and saltpeter. Dry the surface of the meat with paper towels. Tip any liquid from the pot. Rub the spice mixture all over the meat, roll it up and return it to the pot. Cover and leave in a cool place for 9 days, turning the meat daily and rubbing in the spice mixture.

Dry the beef well with paper towels, place it in an ovenproof earthenware pot that will just hold it comfortably and pour the wine over. Cover tightly and cook in a preheated 325° oven for about 3 hours or until the beef is tender.

Remove from the oven and leave in a cool place for about 3 hours. Drain the meat, place it between two boards, and put heavy weights or cans of food on top. Leave in a cool place for 24 hours.

Carve into thin slices and serve with horseradish sauce, beets and thin brown bread and butter or crusty bread, pickled onions and other pickles.

Brown Ragoo of Lamb

The spelling of this dish, an adaptation of the French ragoût, is an example of that country's influence on English culinary matters. Peas or lima beans could be used in place of broad beans.

6 tablespoons unsalted butter, diced	12 small onions
	4 oz button mushrooms
2 lb boned leg of lamb, cut into 1-inch pieces	squeeze of lemon juice
	¾ cup shelled broad beans, cooked, to serve
3 cups brown stock, preferably veal	
	flesh of 2 large firm tomatoes, diced and
1 onion, unpeeled, stuck with 4 cloves	2 tablespoons finely chopped fresh parsley, to garnish
salt and pepper	
3 parsley sprigs	
2 thyme sprigs	SERVES FOUR
2 bay leaves	
small sprig of rosemary	
3 carrots, cut into quarters lengthwise	

Melt 3 tablespoons of the butter in a large heavy frying pan, add the lamb in batches and cook until an even golden brown. Transfer to a casserole using a slotted spoon. Reserve the butter in the pan.

Put the stock in a saucepan with the unpeeled onion, seasoning and herbs and bring to a boil. Pour over the lamb, cover tightly and cook in a preheated 350° oven for about 1 hour, stirring occasionally.

Meanwhile, add another 1 tablespoon butter to the frying pan and melt. Add the carrots and small onions and fry until lightly browned.

Drain on paper towels, then stir into the casserole. Cover tightly again and cook for 30 minutes. Cook the mushrooms in the remaining butter with a squeeze of lemon juice. Drain well.

Remove the onion stuck with cloves from the casserole, then stir in the mushrooms and cook, uncovered, for 10 minutes. Using a slotted spoon, lift the meat and vegetables from the dish and keep warm. Boil the liquid until it is reduced to about 1¾ cups, then pour into a warmed boat.

Arrange the meat on a large warmed serving plate with the vegetables, adding the broad beans, and pour some sauce over. Garnish with the tomato flesh and the parsley. Serve, with the rest of the sauce handed separately.

Lancashire Hot-Pot

This dish – which gets its name from the deep earthenware pot that was traditionally used – has a number of regional variations. In these, ham, mushrooms or even oysters may be added.

6 potatoes, thinly sliced
salt and pepper
8 lamb rib chops
4 lamb's kidneys, skinned, halved and cored
2 onions, thinly sliced

1–1¼ cups chicken stock
about 2 tablespoons drippings or unsalted butter, melted

SERVES FOUR

Grease a deep, earthenware ovenproof pot. Lay about one-third of the potatoes in the bottom and sprinkle with salt and pepper. Pack in four of the chops, followed by two of the kidneys, then half of the onion, seasoning each layer well.

Repeat the layering, finishing with a layer of neatly overlapping potato slices. Pour in sufficient stock to half-fill the pot, then brush the potato covering with melted drippings or butter.

Cook in a preheated 425° oven for 30 minutes, then reduce the temperature to 275°, cover and cook for 2 hours. Increase the heat to 400°, uncover the pot and cook for a further 30 minutes.

Braised Beef with Chestnuts and Celery

This well-flavored casserole, which dates from the eighteenth century, would have been made in the late autumn and winter when both celery and fresh chestnuts were available. Nowadays, it can be made at any time of the year using, where necessary, canned chestnuts.

18 chestnuts, fresh or drained, unsweetened canned
2 tablespoons beef drippings or bacon fat
2 bacon slices, chopped
2 lb beef for stew, cut into cubes
1 onion, chopped
1 tablespoon all-purpose flour
1¼ cups brown ale or dark beer
1¼ cups brown stock, preferably veal
pinch of grated nutmeg
juice and finely grated rind of 1 orange
salt and pepper
3 celery stalks, chopped
finely chopped fresh parsley, to garnish

SERVES FOUR TO SIX

Slit the skins of fresh chestnuts, then cook in simmering water for about 7 minutes. Peel off the thick outer skin and thin inner skin while still warm, removing from the water one at a time.

Melt the drippings or bacon fat in a flameproof casserole, add the bacon and beef in batches and cook, stirring occasionally, until browned. Remove the meat with a slotted spoon and drain thoroughly on paper towels.

Add the onion to the casserole and fry, stirring, until softened. Drain off most of the fat and reserve. Return the meat to the casserole, sprinkle in the flour and cook, stirring, for 1–2 minutes.

Stir in the brown ale, stock, nutmeg, orange juice and half the rind, and the seasoning. Bring to a boil, stir well to dislodge the sediment, then add the fresh chestnuts. Cover tightly with foil and a lid and cook in a preheated 325° oven for about 45 minutes.

Meanwhile, heat the reserved fat in a saucepan, add the celery and fry lightly. Add to the casserole after the 45 minutes cooking time, recover and cook for about 1 hour. (If using canned chestnuts, add them after 30 minutes, recover the casserole and continue cooking for the remaining 30 minutes.)

Serve with the remaining orange rind and the parsley sprinkled over the top.

BROWN RAGOO OF LAMB (page 42)

Boiled Mutton with Caper Sauce

Mutton is the flesh from a lamb that has lived past its first birthday. It is difficult to find nowadays as it is popularly believed to be too fatty and inferior. However, it does have a good flavor and is well worth using for this recipe – excess fat can easily be trimmed. Lamb can be used as an alternative.

5 lb leg of mutton (or lamb)	*Sauce*
	2 tablespoons unsalted butter
salt	1½ teaspoons all-purpose flour
2 onions, halved	
3–4 carrots, halved lengthwise if large	1 egg yolk
2 celery stalks, halved lengthwise	¼ cup heavy cream
	1–2 tablespoons chopped large capers
1 leek, halved lengthwise	
2 bay leaves	finely chopped lemon rind, to garnish
6 black peppercorns, lightly crushed	
long strip of lemon rind	SERVES SIX

Put the meat into a large saucepan, add just enough water to cover and a sprinkling of salt. Bring to a boil, remove the scum from the surface and add the vegetables, bay leaves, peppercorns and lemon rind. Cover and simmer for 2½–3 hours until the meat is very tender. Transfer to a warmed plate and keep warm.

Melt half the butter, stir in the flour and cook for 1–2 minutes. Measure off 2 cups of the cooking liquid and gradually stir into the flour. Bring to a boil, stirring, then simmer until reduced to about 1 cup and slightly thickened.

Blend the egg yolk with the cream, blend in a little of the stock then pour back into the remaining stock and heat gently, stirring, until the sauce thickens – do not allow to boil. Stir in the capers and remaining butter. Adjust the seasoning, if necessary. Pour into a sauceboat and sprinkle the lemon rind over.

Serve the mutton, or lamb, carved into slices accompanied by the sauce.

Shepherd's Pie

Controversy surrounds this dish – should the meat be lamb or beef, should it be cooked or raw, when is the dish a shepherd's pie and when a cottage pie or are they the same? And the variety in the recipes is enormous – some are very simple and basic, others, like this one, have more flavor and character.

2 tablespoons unsalted butter	salt and pepper
1 onion, finely chopped	*Topping*
1 lb lean ground round	14 oz potatoes, cut into chunks
1 cup chopped mushrooms	½ lb celeriac, cut into chunks
1 tablespoon tomato paste	3 tablespoons unsalted butter, diced
⅔ cup red wine	
⅔ cup brown stock, preferably veal	2 eggs, separated
1 tablespoon finely chopped fresh tarragon or 1½ teaspoons dried	SERVES FOUR

Melt the butter, add the onion and cook over a moderate heat until beginning to soften. Add the beef and cook, stirring frequently, until browned. Stir in the mushrooms, tomato paste, wine, stock, tarragon and seasoning. Cook gently for about 25 minutes, stirring occasionally.

Meanwhile, prepare the topping. Simmer the potatoes and celeriac until tender. Drain well and purée in a blender or food processor. Return to the rinsed out pan and heat gently, stirring, until dry. Beat in the butter, egg yolks and seasoning. Beat the egg whites until stiff, then fold into the purée.

Pour the meat into a deep 5-cup baking dish and cover with the potato. Bake in a preheated 400° oven for about 30 minutes until the top is golden.

Parson's Venison

Marinating a leg of lamb in lightly spiced red wine transforms the meat into a more full-flavored dish reminiscent of venison.

2 tablespoons meat drippings or bacon fat	*Marinade*
	1 cup red wine
1 small onion, finely chopped	6 tablespoons tawny port
1 cup chopped mushrooms	6 juniper berries, crushed
½ cup chopped cooked ham	¼ teaspoon ground allspice
2 tablespoons snipped chives	2 tablespoons vegetable oil
salt and pepper	3 tablespoons red wine vinegar
4–4½ lb leg of lamb, boned	1 bay leaf
	¼ teaspoon freshly grated nutmeg

SERVES FOUR TO SIX

Melt half the drippings or bacon fat, add the onion and mushrooms and cook, stirring frequently, until the onions are soft but not browned. Stir in the ham, chives and seasoning and leave to cool.

Season the lamb inside and out with black pepper, then spread the onion mixture over the inside. Roll up tightly and tie securely. Place in a casserole or large dish.

Mix the marinade ingredients together, pour over the lamb, cover and leave in a cool place for 24 hours, turning the roast over occasionally. Remove the meat from the marinade, drain and dry well on paper towels.

Melt the remaining drippings or butter in a flameproof casserole. Add the meat and brown on all sides over medium to high heat.

Pour in the marinade, bring almost to the boil, cover then cook in a preheated 350° oven for 1¾–2 hours until the meat is tender, basting occasionally with the marinade.

Transfer the meat to a warmed plate. Skim the fat from the surface of the liquid, then boil the liquid rapidly until reduced and slightly thickened. Season and serve with the meat.

Oxtail Stew

This stew can be served as it is, straight from the pot with carrots, small onions and leeks.

2 tablespoons beef
   drippings or unsalted
   butter
¼ cup chopped bacon
1 large or 2 small oxtails,
   chopped
1 large onion, finely
   chopped
2 carrots, chopped
1 celery stalk, chopped
1 large leek, chopped
bouquet garni of 1 bay
   leaf, sprig of thyme,
   4 parsley sprigs and a
   sprig of lovage
salt and pepper
1¼ cups brown ale or
   dark beer

1¼ cups brown stock,
   preferably veal
finely chopped fresh
   parsley, to garnish

Dumplings
¾ cup self-rising flour
salt and pepper
4 tablespoons shredded
   suet or cold diced
   butter
½ tsp prepared white
   horseradish (optional)
2 tablespoons water
1 cup brown stock,
   preferably veal, or
   water

SERVES FOUR

Heat the drippings or butter in a large flameproof casserole or heavy-based saucepan, add the bacon and oxtail pieces, a few at a time, and cook until beginning to brown. Remove with a slotted spoon and reserve.

   Add the vegetables to the casserole or pan and cook over a low heat for about 3 minutes, stirring frequently, until the onion is beginning to soften but not brown.

   Return the oxtail and bacon to the vegetables. Add the bouquet garni, seasoning, ale and stock and bring to a boil. Reduce the heat so the liquid barely

moves, cover tightly and cook slowly for 2½–3 hours until the oxtail is very tender. Skim all fat off the surface.

   About 25 minutes before the end of the cooking, combine all the ingredients for the dumplings except the stock and mix to a soft, but not sticky, dough with the water.

   Divide into eight pieces and roll into small balls using floured hands. Bring the stock or water to a boil in a large saucepan; season if using water. Add the dumplings and poach for 15–20 minutes until cooked. Remove from the pan with a slotted spoon, draining well. Place the dumplings on top of the stew and sprinkle with parsley. Serve at once.

CROWN ROAST OF LAMB (page 53)

Traditional Roasts

THE roasts of England are famed throughout the world. Prior to the middle of the nineteenth century they were cooked over an open fire on a spit, with the spit being rotated by hand. In Tudor times, dogs were used, with clockwork mechanisms being introduced in the late eighteenth century. Roasting in the oven did not become an accepted and common practice until the introduction of gas and electric stoves.

The best roast meat comes from a large cut so a roast is an obvious choice to serve when you have guests to feed. English roasts all have their traditional accompaniments – roast beef and Yorkshire pudding or horseradish sauce, lamb with mint sauce, and pork with apple-sauce.

Roast Beef and Yorkshire Puddings

Purists claim that Yorkshire pudding should be cooked beneath the meat, in the same pan so that it absorbs the maximum flavor, but, when made in this way, it will not be as light and crisp as when cooked separately. Using really hot fat helps to ensure light, crisp puddings. If preferred, a single large pudding can be made, but it will take about 35–40 minutes to cook.

Serve with mustard or horseradish sauce (see page 51) and roast potatoes (see page 71).

6 lb standing rib roast, with 3 ribs	pinch of salt
pepper	1 egg, beaten
1 cup red wine	½ cup milk
	½ cup water
Yorkshire puddings	SERVES FOUR TO SIX
¾ cup all-purpose flour	

To make the Yorkshire pudding batter, sift the flour and salt into a bowl. Form a well in the center, then pour in the egg and gradually draw in the flour. Add the milk and water and mix to a smooth batter. Leave to stand for 1–2 hours.

Sprinkle pepper over the beef, place on a rack in a roasting pan, then roast in a preheated 425° oven for

20 minutes. Reduce the temperature to 375° and continue roasting for 15–20 minutes per pound for medium rare meat. Cook for 15 minutes less for rare meat; cook for 15 minutes longer for well done.

Ten minutes before the end of the cooking, pour off the surplus fat and put a little of it into 12 individual muffin tins. Place in the hottest part of the oven for 5 minutes until really hot.

When the meat is done, leave it in a warm place, still on the rack and increase the oven temperature to 425°. Beat the batter, pour into the tins and cook for 15–20 minutes until risen, crisp and golden.

Place the roasting pan over a moderate heat and gradually stir the wine into the cooking juices, dislodging the sediment in the bottom of the pan. Bring to a boil and bubble for a few minutes. Season and pour into a warmed sauceboat.

Serve the beef with the Yorkshire puddings and with the gravy handed separately.

Roast Sirloin with Horseradish Sauce

This classic English dish is reputed to have been knighted by an English king after he had dined particularly well off a roasted loin of beef. For a meal "fit for a king" serve with Yorkshire puddings (see page 50) and roast potatoes (see page 71).

2½ lb boneless rump or
  sirloin tip roast
¾ cup red wine
⅔ cup brown stock,
  preferably veal
salt and pepper

Sauce
⅔ cup heavy cream
3 tablespoons freshly
  grated horseradish
about 1½ tablespoons
  lemon juice
¼–½ teaspoon prepared
  English mustard
salt and white pepper
pinch of sugar (optional)

SERVES FOUR

Place the meat, fat side up, on a rack placed in a roasting pan. Roast in a preheated 450° oven for 15 minutes, then reduce the temperature to 325° and roast for about a further 40 minutes for rare beef, basting once or twice.

Meanwhile, blend all the ingredients for the sauce and spoon into a serving bowl.

Leave the beef, still on the rack, in a warm place to rest. Drain off the excess fat from the roasting pan. Place the pan over a medium heat and stir in the red wine, dislodging the sediment stuck in the bottom of the pan.

Boil until almost completely evaporated, then stir in the stock and boil until reduced to a scant 1 cup. Season and pour into a sauceboat. Serve the beef accompanied by the gravy and horseradish sauce.

Roast Pork

For the traditional crackling, ask the butcher to leave the skin on the pork roast. Score right through the skin with a firm, sharp knife, following the grain of the meat, then rub the skin with vegetable or olive oil and coarse salt before cooking.

3½ lb pork loin roast, vegetable oil and coarse salt
rosemary sprig
6 large tart apples
salt and pepper
⅔ cup dry white wine (optional)

⅔ cup brown stock, preferably veal
watercress sprigs, to garnish

SERVES FOUR TO SIX

Rub the skin of the pork with oil and then sprinkle with coarse salt. Place the rosemary on a rack in a roasting pan, put the pork on top and roast in a preheated 350° oven for 2 hours.

Core the apples, season them inside and make a shallow cut through the skin around the apples about one-third of the way down. Place in a pan or dish and baste with some of the fat from the pork. Cook on a lower shelf for the last 30 minutes of the cooking time.

Keep the pork warm on a rack. Drain off most of the fat from the roasting pan, leaving the meat juices. Stir in the wine, if using, dislodging the sediment. Boil until almost completely evaporated. Stir in stock and boil for 2–3 minutes. Strain into a sauceboat.

Arrange the apples around the pork, garnish with watercress and serve accompanied by the gravy.

Guard of Honor with Mint Sauce

If ordered in advance, the butcher will trim the racks of lamb. If the meat is from a very young lamb and the chops small it will probably be necessary to allow four per person.

2 racks of lamb containing 6 chops each
½ cup red wine
⅔ cup brown stock, preferably veal
salt and pepper
lima or broad beans and new potatoes, to serve
red currant jelly (see page 93), to serve

Sauce
¼ cup finely chopped fresh mint
3 tablespoons boiling water
2 tablespoons sugar
¼ cup white wine or wine vinegar
salt and pepper

SERVES FOUR

Trim each chop bone to a depth of 2 inches, then interlace the bones, fat side outwards, to form an arch. Tie the meat at intervals along the length and weave string between the bones to keep the roast in shape. Protect the tips of the bones with foil.

Place on a rack in a roasting pan and roast in a preheated 450° oven for 10 minutes, then reduce the temperature to 350° and roast for a further 25 minutes, basting occasionally.

To make the sauce, put the mint in a bowl, pour over the boiling water and leave for 20 minutes. Stir in the sugar, wine or wine vinegar and seasoning.

Remove the foil and leave the lamb, still on the rack, to rest for 15 minutes. Drain off the fat from the roasting pan. Stir in the wine and boil for a few minutes, then stir in the stock and boil for

2–3 minutes. Season, then pour into a sauceboat.

Transfer the lamb to a warmed serving plate and remove the trussing strings. Serve accompanied by the gravy, mint sauce, lima or broad beans, new potatoes and red currant jelly.

Crown Roast of Lamb

Order the roast 2 or 3 days in advance if you would like the butcher to prepare it for you. Ask him to include the trimmings with the roast. The stuffing may be cooked in the center of the lamb but the cooking time will need to be longer, and the meat will not be rare. The apple and mint stuffing used here is soft and moist – for a firmer stuffing, double the quantity of breadcrumbs and add an egg.

2 racks of lamb
   containing 6 chops each
1 tablespoon unsalted
   butter
1 small onion, halved
1 leek, halved
1 carrot, halved
1 celery stalk, halved
5 black peppercorns
1 cup dry white wine
1½ quarts water
salt

Stuffing
3 tablespoons unsalted
   butter

2 shallots, finely chopped
1¼ lb tart apples, peeled,
   cored and chopped
   (about 4 cups)
1 cup fresh breadcrumbs
2 tablespoons finely
   chopped fresh mint or 3
   teaspoons dried
salt and pepper
baby vegetables – peas,
   small turnips, carrots,
   new potatoes, snow
   peas, to serve

SERVES FOUR

Trim each chop bone to a depth of 2 inches. Bend the joints around, fat side inwards, and sew together using strong thread or fine string to form a crown.

Melt the butter in a saucepan, add the lamb trimmings and cook over a moderate heat until the fat melts and they color very slightly.

Stir in the vegetables and cook for 2–3 minutes, stirring occasionally. Stir in the peppercorns, wine, water and salt. Bring to a boil, remove the scum from the surface, then simmer for 2–3 hours, removing the scum occasionally.

Strain the stock, leave to cool, then remove the fat from the surface. Boil the stock until reduced to about 1¼ cups.

Place the crown roast on a rack in a roasting pan and cover the exposed bones with foil. Roast in a preheated 425° oven for 15 minutes, then reduce the temperature to 350°. Tip any fat from the roasting pan and brush the roast with some of the stock. Return the roast to the oven and cook for 45–50 minutes, basting two or three times with the stock.

Meanwhile, prepare the stuffing. Heat 2 tablespoons of the butter, add the shallots, cover and cook for 3–4 minutes, shaking the pan occasionally until the shallots are softened but not colored.

Stir in the apples and cook, stirring occasionally, until softened. Remove from the heat and stir in the breadcrumbs, mint and seasoning. Spoon into a buttered dish, dot the remaining butter on the top and cook in the oven for about 30 minutes.

Keep the lamb warm, still on the rack. Drain off the excess fat from the roasting pan, leaving the juices behind. Stir in the remaining stock, dislodging the sediment. Bring to a boil and boil for 2–3 minutes.

Place the crown roast on a warmed serving plate, remove the foil, and spoon the stuffing into the center. Pour the gravy into a small warmed boat and arrange baby vegetables around the meat.

Poultry and Game Dishes

AT ONE time almost every household in the town, village and country kept at least a few chickens and these, along perhaps with some geese and ducks, would be the responsibility of the lady of the house, whether the house was a manor or a small cottage and whether she attended to the birds herself or directed someone else.

The birds provided eggs both for the household, and in country districts a little extra income. Generally the birds were not killed until they had ceased to lay economically, by which time they would be old, tough and frequently a little stringy. They would, however, have a good flavor and could be made into tasty dishes if cooked slowly. Young, tender birds were only killed if they were poor layers, or for a special occasion if the family could afford it.

The birds would roam around scratching for food, and different breeds became crossed with each other to produce new strains. By the 1850s some selective breeding experiments were begin-

ning to take place to produce breeds with specific characteristics, some for table use and some as layers. To keep them separate they were housed in cages and runs which, by the end of the nineteenth century, led to the first commercial poultry farms, and the beginnings of the poultry industry existing today.

→ Game →

Game (birds and animals that are hunted and killed for sport as well as eating) was the province of the master of the house, from the king downwards. Since Saxon times the Crown had earmarked game preserves for itself and these lands were so extensive by the reign of Henry II, in the twelfth century, that they covered about one third of England. However, despite the severity of the punishments for poaching, which at times have been death or transportation, much game found its way onto the tables of those not included in the exclusive band of authorized consumers.

Partridges "Stewed" with Red Wine and Anchovies

Anchovies used to be used quite frequently in meat, poultry and game dishes to enhance and enrich the dish without being allowed to dominate the other flavors. Cooked in this way older partridges – or other game birds, squab, hare or venison – become deliciously tender. The dish should traditionally be served with lima beans and Brussels sprouts for a warming winter dish.

1 onion, finely chopped	4 tablespoons unsalted
white part of 1 long thin	butter
leek, finely chopped	2 cups Bordeaux or
1 small carrot, finely	similar red wine
chopped	salt and pepper
bouquet garni of	croûtons dipped in
4 parsley sprigs, sprig	chopped parsley, to
of thyme and a small	garnish
sprig of sage	lima beans and Brussels
2 partridges	sprouts, to serve
2 cups game stock	
2 anchovy fillets	SERVES FOUR

Mix the vegetables together in a heavy flameproof casserole. Add the bouquet garni and partridges. Pour in the stock and bring to simmering point. Cover with aluminum foil and a lid and cook gently for about 1 hour.

Pound the anchovies with half the butter, then add to the casserole with the wine and seasoning. Bring to simmering point again, then recover with the foil and lid and cook for a further 1½ hours.

Transfer the partridges to a warmed serving plate and keep warm. Discard the bouquet garni and boil the liquid until reduced and slightly thickened. Strain through a sieve, if wished, and reheat gently. Over a low heat, stir in the remaining butter and adjust the seasoning.

Pour the sauce over the partridges. Garnish with the croûtons and serve with lima beans and Brussels sprouts.

Salmi of Pheasant

This is a classic example of a very good, traditional English dish, a salomene, having its name changed to a French one for reasons of culinary snobbery. Although it can be made with leftover pheasant, or other game, it is best to use birds that have been specifically cooked for this recipe. Preparation is quicker if 2 cups pre-prepared game stock is used.

2 young pheasants
salt and pepper
2 thyme sprigs
2 bacon slices
1 onion, halved
1 large carrot, quartered
2 cups red wine
5 cups brown stock, preferably veal
bouquet garni of sprig of parsley, sprig of thyme, small sprig of rosemary and a bay leaf

5 tablespoons unsalted butter
2 shallots, finely chopped
1 tablespoon all-purpose flour
4 oz mushrooms
croûtons and chopped fresh parsley, to garnish

SERVES FOUR

Season the pheasants, place a sprig of thyme in the cavity of each and tie a slice of bacon over the breasts. Place in a roasting pan just large enough to hold them and roast in a preheated 450° oven for 25 minutes. Leave the oven on.

Remove the bacon and trussing strings. Remove and reserve the skin and cut up the birds. Carefully remove the meat from the bones and carcass. Place the meat in a casserole.

Chop the bones and skin and put into a roasting pan with the onion and carrot. Cook in the oven for about 10 minutes, stirring occasionally, until browned. Tip the bones, skin and vegetables into a large saucepan. Stir 1¼ cups of the wine into the roasting pan to dislodge the sediment, bring to a boil then pour into the saucepan.

Add the veal stock, bring to a boil, remove the scum from the surface, add the bouquet garni and simmer for about 2 hours, removing the scum from the surface occasionally.

Strain through a sieve, pressing down on the bones and vegetables to extract as much liquid as possible. Measure the liquid – there should be about 2 cups.

Melt 3 tablespoons of the butter in a saucepan, add the shallots, cover and cook, shaking the pan occasionally, until softened but not browned. Stir in the flour then gradually stir in the stock. Bring to a boil, stirring, then simmer for about 20 minutes.

Meanwhile, boil the remaining wine until reduced to 1 tablespoon. Cook the mushrooms in the remaining butter.

Stir the sauce into the reduced wine and bring to a boil. Adjust the seasoning. Pour over the pheasant, moving the pieces carefully to make sure they are all covered with the sauce. Stir in the mushrooms. Cover and heat through in a 350° oven for about 15–20 minutes.

Transfer to a warmed serving plate and garnish with the croûtons and parsley.

SALMI OF PHEASANT (above)

Cornish Caudle Chicken Pie

Caudle refers to the cream and egg mixture that is poured into the pie near the end of the cooking. The quantity of pastry will give just a thin covering, a larger amount can be used if preferred.

4 tablespoons unsalted butter	⅔ cup milk
1 onion, finely chopped	⅔ cup sour cream
4 chicken legs, about 4 oz each, boned	½ lb puff pastry
	beaten egg, for glazing
⅓ cup finely chopped fresh parsley	⅔ cup heavy cream
	1 egg, beaten
4 scallions, chopped	
salt and pepper	SERVES FOUR

Melt half the butter in a frying pan, add the onion and cook over a low heat, stirring occasionally, until softened but not browned. Transfer to a deep 5-cup pie dish or casserole using a slotted spoon.

Add the remaining butter to the pan, add the chicken and cook until evenly browned. Arrange on top of the onion in a single layer. Stir the parsley, scallions, seasoning, milk and sour cream into the pan and bring to a boil. Simmer for 2–3 minutes, then pour over the chicken.

Cover with foil and cook in a preheated 350° oven for about 30 minutes. Remove from the oven and leave to cool.

Meanwhile, roll out the pastry on a lightly floured surface until about 1 inch larger all around than the pie dish. Leave the pastry to relax while the filling is cooling.

Cut off a strip from all around the edge of the pastry. Place the strip on the rim of the pie dish, moisten, then place the pastry lid on top. Crimp the edges, make a small hole in the top and insert a small funnel of foil.

Brush the top of the pie with beaten egg and bake in a preheated 425° oven for 15–20 minutes until a light golden brown. Reduce the temperature to 350°.

Beat the cream into the egg, then strain into a pitcher and pour into the pie through the foil funnel. Remove the funnel, shake the dish to distribute the cream and return the pie to the oven for about 5 minutes. Remove from the oven and leave to stand in a warm place for 5–10 minutes before serving warm, or leave to cool completely and serve cold.

Squab in a Pot with Plums

Squabs are particularly plentiful in the countryside in the autumn, especially in corn growing regions, just at the time when plums are ripe. This dish from Kent happily combines the two.

1 tablespoon unsalted butter	1 teaspoon finely chopped fresh thyme or ½ teaspoon dried
4 squabs	
2 teaspoons all-purpose flour seasoned with a pinch of grated nutmeg	½ teaspoon finely chopped fresh sage
	½ cup port wine
1 onion, chopped	1 lb purple plums, halved and pitted
2 cloves	
1 teaspoon finely chopped fresh rosemary or ½ teaspoon dried	SERVES FOUR

Melt the butter in a frying pan. Coat the squabs lightly in the flour, then add to the pan and fry, turning occasionally, until lightly browned. Transfer to an ovenproof casserole.

Stir the onion into the frying pan and fry gently until beginning to soften. Spoon over the squabs and sprinkle the cloves and herbs over the top.

Stir the port into the frying pan, bring to a boil, then pour over the squabs. Arrange the plums over the top. Cover tightly and cook in a preheated 325° oven for 1½ hours or until the squabs are tender.

Transfer the squabs and plums to a warmed large serving platter. Boil the juices to thicken them and concentrate the flavor. Pour over the squabs.

Roast Haunch of Venison

Venison is a very lean meat. Marinating, then wrapping in a simple flour or "huff" paste, help to keep it moist and succulent.

1 small haunch of venison, about 4 lb	about 1½ cups water
¼ cup vegetable oil	4 tablespoons unsalted butter, softened
3 shallots, chopped	red currant jelly (see page 93) or Cumberland sauce (see page 94), to serve
1 carrot, chopped	
1 bay leaf	
sprig of marjoram	
2 parsley sprigs	
10 black peppercorns, lightly crushed	SERVES FOUR
8 juniper berries	
2½ cups red wine	
4 cups all-purpose flour	

Put the venison into a large dish. Mix the oil, shallots, carrot, bay leaf, marjoram, parsley, peppercorns, juniper berries and wine together and pour over the venison. Cover and leave in a cool place for 24 hours, basting the meat occasionally and turning it over two or three times. Remove the venison from the marinade, drain and dry it well. Reserve the marinade.

Mix the flour to a stiff paste with the water. Roll out to about ½ inch thick. Spread the butter over the venison, then encase the roast in the paste, dampening the edges and pressing them to seal.

Wrap in brown paper or a double thickness of parchment paper. Place in a roasting pan and cook in a preheated 450° oven for 15 minutes. Reduce the temperature to 325° and cook for 20 minutes per pound.

About 30 minutes before the end of the cooking time, remove and discard the paper and the crust. Raise the oven temperature to 425°, baste the venison with some of the marinade, and complete the cooking, basting twice more.

Transfer to a rack on a warmed plate and keep warm. Place the roasting pan over a moderately high heat, gradually add 1 cup of the marinade, stirring to dislodge the sediment. Bring to a boil and boil for a few minutes. Pour into a warmed sauceboat and serve with the venison accompanied by red currant jelly or Cumberland sauce.

Douce Ame

This recipe is based upon one that appeared in the "Forme of Cury" (Manner of Cookery), one of the earliest collections of manuscript recipes, written about 1390 by Richard II's cooks.

4 lb chicken, cut up	½ teaspoon chopped
all-purpose flour	hyssop (or use an extra
2 tablespoons unsalted	½ sage leaf and a small
butter	pinch of chopped fresh
2½ cups milk	mint)
about 2 tablespoons	½ teaspoon finely
honey	chopped summer
3 tablespoons chopped	savory or ¼ teaspoon
fresh parsley	dried
2 small sage leaves, finely	pinch of ground saffron
chopped or ½ teaspoon	salt and pepper
dried	½ cup pine nuts

SERVES FOUR

Lightly coat the pieces of chicken in flour seasoned with salt and pepper. Melt the butter in a heavy flameproof casserole, add the chicken and cook over a medium heat until golden brown.

Blend the milk, honey, herbs, saffron and seasoning together. Lift the chicken out of the casserole and stir the flavored milk into the juices, dislodging the sediment. Bring to a boil, then add the chicken, turning the pieces to coat them in the liquid. Cover and cook over a low heat for about 40 minutes – the water should barely move.

Lift the pieces of chicken from the liquid and remove the skin. Boil the liquid to reduce it slightly and concentrate the flavor. Adjust the seasoning. Add pine nuts, return chicken to the casserole and serve.

Duckling with Green Peas

This particular recipe for the well-known combination of duckling and green peas is much less fatty than some, yet the vegetables still have plenty of flavor. Use a fresh duckling for the best results. If fresh peas are not available, frozen ones can be substituted. There is no need to blanch them.

4½–5 lb duckling	¼ cup veal stock
3 tablespoons unsalted	2 summer savory sprigs
butter	salt and pepper
12–15 or small onions	
4 cups shelled peas	SERVES FOUR
¼ cup diced smoked	
bacon	

Prick the skin of the duck, taking care not to pierce the flesh. Place on a rack in a roasting pan and cook in a preheated 425° oven for 40 minutes.

Melt the butter in a saucepan, add the onions and cook turning frequently until lightly browned. Blanch the peas for 3 minutes, refresh and drain well. Blanch the bacon for 1 minute, rinse and drain well.

Pour the surplus fat from the roasting pan then stir the stock into the sediment. Mix the peas, bacon, onions and savory together, place around the duck, season the duck and vegetables and cook at 325° for about 20–30 minutes so the breast remains pink.

Serve the duck surrounded by the vegetables and with the cooking juices.

DUCKLING WITH GREEN PEAS (above)

Michaelmas Goose

Queen Elizabeth I ordered that roast goose should be served in commemoration of the defeat of the Spanish Armada on Michaelmas Day (the feast of Saint Michael on September 29). A Michaelmas goose, fattened on the gleanings from the cornfields, was less fatty than a Christmas bird. It was customarily served with other foods available at the same time – the first apples and a special pudding made from corn.

8–10 lb goose	finely grated rind and
salt and pepper	juice of 1 lemon
Stuffing	*Sauce*
4 tablespoons unsalted	1 lb tart apples
butter	2 tablespoons unsalted
2 onions, finely chopped	butter
the goose liver, finely	2–4 tablespoons sugar
chopped	2 cloves or a pinch of
3 tablespoons finely	freshly grated nutmeg
chopped fresh sage or	1 tablespoon water
1 tablespoon dried	
3 cups fresh white	SERVES SIX TO EIGHT
breadcrumbs	

To make the stuffing, melt the butter, add the onions and cook gently, stirring occasionally, until softened but not browned. Stir in the liver and cook until it just begins to stiffen and change color. Remove from the heat and stir in the sage, breadcrumbs, lemon rind and juice and seasoning.

Remove any lumps of fat from the cavity of the goose, then season it well inside and out. Spoon the stuffing into the neck end. Do not pack the stuffing too tightly. If there is too much stuffing, put the extra in a roasting pan and cook in the oven 30 minutes before the end of the cooking time.

Truss the goose neatly, then prick the breasts, sides and legs. Place the bird, breast side up, on a rack in a roasting pan and cook in a preheated 425° oven for 20 minutes.

Turn the goose over. Reduce the temperature to 325° and cook for 1 hour. Turn the goose over again onto its back and cook for about 1 hour until the juices run clear when the thickest part of the leg is pierced with a skewer. Pour off the fat several times during the cooking.

To make the applesauce, peel, core and chop the apples. Put with the butter, sugar, cloves or nutmeg and water in a saucepan, cover and cook gently until soft. Beat to a smooth pureé.

Leave the goose to stand in a warm place for 15 minutes before carving. Serve with the sauce.

Rabbit in the Dairy

This is a sympathetic method of cooking young rabbit that works equally well with chicken pieces. It is pale, but is deliberately left ungarnished so as not to detract from the delicate flavor. Instead, serve it on a colorful plate. Young broad beans and new potatoes cooked in their skins are good accompaniments.

1 small celery stalk, finely	salt and white pepper
chopped	2 fresh bay leaves
1 shallot, finely chopped	1¼ cups milk
2 tablespoons finely	
chopped cooked ham	SERVES FOUR
1 young rabbit, cut up	

Arrange the celery, shallot and ham in a heavy earthenware casserole. Place the pieces of rabbit on top, season and add the bay leaves.

Bring the milk to a boil and pour over the rabbit. Cover tightly and cook in a preheated 325° oven for about 2 hours until the rabbit is tender.

Strain off the cooking liquid and boil to reduce slightly. Taste and adjust the seasoning. Transfer the rabbit, vegetables and ham to a warmed serving plate or dish and pour the liquid over.

Edgurdouce

Conyng (coney or mature rabbit) was very popular in medieval times and is featured in many recipes from that time. It was rated so highly as a meat that it was served at the coronation feast of Henry IV in 1399. This recipe is typical of the sweet spiciness of dishes then. Use dried apricots without added sulfur dioxide.

1¼ cups sweet wine
3 tablespoons red wine
   vinegar
1 cup (6 oz) seedless
   muscatel raisins
1⅓ cups (6 oz) dried
   apricots
1 teaspoon ground ginger
1 teaspoon ground
   cinnamon
a small piece of fresh
   ginger root, very finely
   chopped
4 cloves

4 juniper berries, lightly
   crushed
salt and white pepper
1 young rabbit cut into 4
all-purpose flour, for
   coating
1½ tablespoons olive oil
orange segments, pith
   and peel removed, and
   finely shredded
   preserved ginger, to
   garnish

SERVES FOUR

Gently warm the wine and vinegar to simmering point, then pour over the raisins and apricots in a bowl. Add the spices and seasoning, stir, cover and leave overnight.

Add the rabbit portions to the fruits and liquid, turn them over to coat in the liquid, then cover and leave in a cool place for about 6 hours, turning occasionally.

Dry the rabbit portions with paper towels and coat lightly in flour. Heat the oil in a heavy flameproof casserole, add the rabbit and fry until a light golden brown. Drain on paper towels.

Pour off any excess oil from the casserole, then stir in the wine and fruit and bring to a boil. Return the rabbit to the casserole, cover with foil and a lid and cook for about 40 minutes until the rabbit is tender – the liquid should hardly move.

Transfer the rabbit to a warmed serving plate and keep warm. Boil the liquid until reduced and thickened, then pour over the rabbit.

Serve garnished with orange segments and finely shredded preserved ginger.

Game Pie

A delicious cold pie that is traditionally packed as part of the lunch for shooting parties. It is also ideal for a buffet.

1 pheasant	*Stock*
1 grouse	1 onion, chopped
1 partridge	1 carrot, chopped
1 squab	1 celery stalk, chopped
½ lb slab bacon	⅔ cup white wine
4 oz salt pork	2 cups chicken stock
2 shallots	6 juniper berries
salt and pepper	bouquet garni of 1 bay
	leaf, 4 parsley sprigs,
Marinade	sprig of thyme and
1¼ cups red wine	small sprig of rosemary
2 tablespoons brandy	1 lb hot water crust pastry
¼ cup oil	beaten egg, to glaze
8 juniper berries, crushed	2 teaspoons unflavored
3 parsley sprigs	gelatin
3 thyme sprigs	Cumberland sauce, to
1 bay leaf	serve (page 94)
2 sage leaves	
blade of mace	SERVES EIGHT

Remove and reserve the skin from the birds. Remove and discard the fat. Carefully remove the breasts from each bird with a sharp knife, cutting away as much of the remaining meat as possible from the bones. Cut the meat into approximately ¾-inch pieces. Chop the carcasses and bones.

Grind the bacon, salt pork and shallots together and mix with the game meat. Put in a large earthenware dish. Mix the marinade ingredients together, pour into the dish, stir lightly to mix, cover and leave in a cool place for 24 hours, turning the meat over occasionally.

Meanwhile, put the carcasses, skin and bones into a roasting pan and brown in preheated 425° oven for 20 minutes. Add the onion, carrot and celery for the stock, turning them over to coat in the juices in the pan, and cook for 10 minutes.

Transfer the carcasses, bones and vegetables to a large saucepan. Place the roasting pan over a medium heat, add the wine and stir to dislodge the sediment. Bring to a boil, then pour into the saucepan. Add the stock, juniper berries and bouquet garni and bring to a boil.

Remove the scum from the surface, then simmer for 2 hours, removing the scum occasionally. Pass through a conical strainer. Boil if necessary to reduce to 2 cups.

Leave to cool, then remove the fat from the surface. Drain the liquid from the meats and dry the meats well on paper towels.

Roll out two-thirds of the pastry and use to line the bottom and sides of a 9-inch raised pie mold or hinged pâté mold, leaving a slight overlap all the way around. Spoon the meats into the pastry case, seasoning them well.

Roll out the remaining pastry to form a lid and cover the pie. Press the edges well to seal them, then trim off the excess pastry. Scallop the edges. Make a small hole in the center of the lid and insert a small funnel of foil. Decorate the pie, then brush the top with beaten egg.

Bake in a preheated 400° oven for 20 minutes, then reduce the temperature to 350° and cook for a further 1½ hours. Remove the sides of the mold, or unfasten them. Brush the pie all over with beaten egg and return to the oven for 15–20 minutes. To check if the filling is cooked, insert a skewer into the center of the pie. Leave for 10 seconds, then remove the skewer; it should be hot. If not, brush the pie with more beaten egg and return it to the oven for a further 15 minutes. ☞

CORNISH CAUDLE CHICKEN PIE (page 58)

Leave the pie on a wire rack until almost cold.

Sprinkle the gelatin over a little of the stock and leave for 2 minutes. Stir in the remaining stock and heat gently, stirring, until the gelatin has dissolved. Cool until it is just becoming a light syrupy consistency, then pour through a funnel placed in the lid of the pie.

Leave the pie in a cool place overnight. Return to room temperature 2 hours before serving.

Jugged Hare

This dish gets its name from the earthenware jug-type cooking pot that was used for cooking older, tougher hare for a long time on the hearth beside a large open fire. If you shoot and dress the hare yourself, keep the blood for the sauce.

6 oz bacon, diced (about ¾ cup)
4 tablespoons unsalted butter
1 large hare, cut up
12 small onions
2 celery stalks, sliced
2 carrots, chopped
bouquet garni of 1 bay leaf, small sprig of rosemary, 6 parsley sprigs, sprig of thyme and 2 sage leaves
blade of mace,
    6 peppercorns and
    6 cloves, tied in
    cheesecloth

salt and pepper
⅔ cup red wine
6 tablespoons ruby port wine
1 cup game or meat stock
lemon juice (optional)
croûtons and parsley sprigs, to garnish
red currant jelly (see page 93) and boiled potatoes, to serve

SERVES SIX

Heat the bacon gently in a heavy flameproof casserole until the fat runs, then add the butter. When it has melted, add the hare pieces and cook until an even light mahogany brown. Remove with a slotted spoon and keep warm.

Add the vegetables to the casserole and fry, stirring occasionally, until the onions are lightly browned.

Pour off any excess fat and return the hare to the casserole. Add the bouquet garni, cheesecloth bag and seasoning. Cover tightly with foil then a lid.

Stand the casserole in a larger one containing sufficient boiling water to come just above the height of the ingredients in the first pot. Cover tightly and simmer gently, replenishing the water as necessary, for about 3 hours until the hare is tender.

Transfer the hare and vegetables to a warmed serving plate and keep warm. Strain the juices, add the wine and port and boil until reduced to 5 tablespoons. Add the stock and simmer for 5 minutes. Reduce the heat.

Allow a little of the liquid to cool, then stir it into the blood if you have it. Heat gently, stirring until thickened but do not allow it to boil. Season with salt, pepper and lemon juice, if necessary.

Spoon over the hare and garnish. Serve with red currant jelly and potatoes.

Vegetables

IN A society that considers the consumption of flesh an indication of wealth and prestige, vegetables have always played a secondary role to game, meat and poultry.

However vegetables did formerly play a larger part in the diet of country folk and the poor than they do today, and even in the homes of the ordinary middle classes vegetables would be made into tasty family dishes such as ragoos. Any roots, leafy vegetables or shoots that grew wild, or could be cultivated easily on a plot of land, were a valued source of food.

Onions, leeks, garlic and cabbage were the most common early vegetables, with herbs being used far more widely, and in much greater variety than is common practice today – some early salads were composed almost exclusively of different types of fresh herbs.

With the increase of traveling, more and more varieties of vegetables were introduced from abroad. Some that Britons consider quite unusual or new today were in popular use years ago, such as globe and Jerusalem artichokes, asparagus and salsify. Celery and cucumber were cooked for serving as hot vegetable dishes.

Commercial market gardening began in the seventeenth century around London and the southeast, but did not really begin to develop on any scale until the eighteenth and nineteenth centuries. It remained restricted to the southern counties until improved transportation enabled produce to be carried further north.

An Eighteenth Century Fine Salad

In the days when salads often contained meat, fish or chicken, this would have been considered a very simple salad. But even so, it would have been arranged attractively.

1 head crisp lettuce
2 large or 4 small cooked
 artichoke bottoms,
 diced
1½ lb thin asparagus
 spears, cooked and
 trimmed to 4 inches
crisp croûtons fried in
 unsalted butter, to
 serve
finely chopped fresh
 chervil or parsley and
 chervil or parsley
 sprigs, to garnish

Dressing
1 small egg yolk
2 small lightly hard-
 boiled egg yolks,
 sieved
salt and white pepper
pinch of cayenne
pinch of sugar
about 2 teaspoons lemon
 juice or herb vinegar
⅔ cup heavy cream

SERVES FOUR TO SIX

First prepare the dressing. Stir the raw egg yolk into the hard-boiled egg yolks, then stir in the seasonings, sugar and lemon juice or vinegar. Gradually stir in the cream. Taste and add more lemon juice or vinegar and seasonings, if necessary.

Wash and dry the lettuce leaves and arrange on a large platter with the artichoke bottoms, and asparagus spears. Place the dressing in the center.

Scatter warm croûtons over and garnish with finely chopped chervil and sprigs of chervil.

AN EIGHTEENTH CENTURY FINE SALAD (above)

Bubble and Squeak

The story behind the name of this dish is that the boiled beef and boiled vegetables originally used bubbled in the water and squeaked when they were fried.

3 tablespoons beef
   drippings or bacon fat
4 or 8 slices of boiled or
   otherwise cooked beef
1 onion, finely chopped
1 lb potatoes, cooked and
   mashed (about 2 cups)

½ lb cooked cabbage,
   finely chopped (about
   2½ cups)
salt and pepper

SERVES FOUR

Heat the drippings or bacon fat in a frying pan. Add the slices of beef and cook until lightly browned on both sides. Drain on paper towels and keep warm.

Add the onion to the pan and cook, stirring frequently, until softened. Remove with a slotted spoon and mix with the potatoes, cabbage and seasoning. Spoon this mixture into the frying pan and flatten it out to make a large flat cake.

Fry over medium heat for about 15 minutes until browned underneath. Turn the cake over and brown the other side. Cut into wedges or pieces and serve beside the beef.

Pease Pudding

Pease pudding, from the north of England, is served with pork or ham. Instead of the final baking used here, the purée can be returned to the cloth and boiled for a further 45 minutes. Cold pease pudding can be sliced and fried in bacon fat.

1 cup (½ lb) yellow split
   peas, soaked overnight
   and drained
¼ cup chopped bacon
1 onion, quartered
1 carrot, halved
bouquet garni of 1 bay
   leaf, 4 parsley sprigs,
   sprig of thyme and
   2 sage leaves

4 tablespoons unsalted
   butter
1 egg, beaten
pinch of sugar
salt and pepper

SERVES FOUR TO SIX

Tie the peas in a cloth leaving plenty of room for them to swell. Put into a large saucepan with the bacon, onion, carrot and bouquet garni. Cover with water, bring to a boil and boil for 10 minutes, then lower the heat, cover and simmer the pudding for about 2½ hours.

Tip the peas out of the cloth and press through a sieve, using a wooden spoon.

Beat in half the butter, the egg, a pinch of sugar and the seasoning. Spoon into a buttered dish, dot with the remaining butter and bake in a preheated 400° oven for 30 minutes.

Pan Haggerty

A tasty potato dish from Northumberland which can be served for supper.

¼ cup beef drippings or
  bacon fat
1 lb firm potatoes, sliced
  very thinly
½ lb onions, thinly sliced

1 cup grated Cheddar
  cheese
salt and pepper

SERVES FOUR

Melt the drippings or bacon fat in a large, heavy frying pan. Remove the pan from the heat and arrange the potatoes, onions and cheese in alternate layers, starting and ending with potatoes, and seasoning the layers with salt and pepper.

Cook for about 30 minutes over low heat at first, then over higher heat so that the underside of the mixture browns.

Place under a hot broiler for 5–10 minutes to brown the top layer of potatoes.

Roast Potatoes

For crisp roast potatoes, they must be thoroughly dry and put into very hot fat.

1¼ lb potatoes, cut into
  halves or large chunks

fat from the roast, or
  drippings

SERVES FOUR

Cook the potatoes in lightly salted simmering water for about 7 minutes. Drain well and dry on paper towels.

Pour some of the fat from around the roast into a separate pan, or put the drippings into the pan and return to the oven so that it becomes really hot.

Put the potatoes into the fat, turn them over so they are coated in fat and roast in a preheated 400°–425° oven for about 40 minutes until crisp and golden.

Puddings

O THE English, pudding generally refers to hot, sweet dishes such as crumbles, rice and other cereal puddings, baked and steamed sponge cakes, suet mixtures, pies, tarts and other pastries, crêpes and fritters. It may also include all cold sweet dishes that are served at the end of a meal – trifle, fruit fools, syllabubs, gelatins and even ice creams, but these are normally called desserts rather than puddings.

The very first puddings and pies were, in fact, savory dishes, although many contained sweet ingredients, spices and fruits. But by the middle of the seventeenth century they began to become more sweet as sugar became cheaper and more readily available.

By the beginning of the eighteenth century, pudding usually meant a dish that was based on sugar, flour and suet, often with fruits, spices and eggs added. Under the patronage of George I, nicknamed the pudding king, recipes for very sweet, rich and often heavy, puddings increased enormously, with nearly every town or village, profession or occupation, notable occasion and even battle having a pudding named after it.

Until the beginning of the nineteenth century, puddings and pies were served as part of the second and third courses alongside savory dishes, but with the gradual defining of courses, they began to take their place at the end of the meal, joining the elaborate molded sweets and gelatins, the fanciful confections and cakes, the carved creations of iced desserts, preserves and fruits, that had their heyday with the French influence during Victoria's reign.

BOODLES ORANGE FOOL (page 74)

Port Wine Gelatin

Prior to the introduction of commercial gelatin mixes, molded gelatins were serious desserts, and in the fifteenth and sixteenth centuries they were often set in elaborate molds and served, shimmering, on silver salvers.

rind of 1 lemon and 1 orange in long strips	1 cinnamon stick
juice of 1 lemon	1 egg white, lightly beaten
⅔ cup sugar	the shells of 2 eggs crushed
1 cup and 2 tablespoons water	1¼ cups ruby port wine
1 tablespoon unflavored gelatin	SERVES FOUR
1 tablespoon red currant jelly (see page 93)	

Scald all the equipment to be used for the gelatin.

Place the lemon and orange rind, lemon juice, sugar and scant 1 cup water in a saucepan and heat gently, stirring, until the sugar has dissolved.

Sprinkle the gelatin over the remaining water in a bowl and leave to soften for 2 minutes. Stand in a saucepan of hot water and stir until the gelatin has dissolved.

Stir into the sugar syrup with the red currant jelly and cinnamon. Whisk in the egg white and shells and continue whisking until the mixture comes to the boil.

Stop whisking as the foam begins to rise and remove the pan from the heat. Return the pan to the heat and repeat this procedure twice, allowing the foam to rise and fall without any further whisking. Cool for 10 minutes.

Pour the gelatin through a jelly bag or sieve lined with a double thickness of cheesecloth, into a bowl – do not press it through or it will cloud the gelatin, but allow it to drip undisturbed.

Stir in the port, then pour into a dampened 2½-cup mold and leave to set in a cool place for at least 4 hours.

To serve, dip the mold up to the rim in hot water for 5 seconds, then place a plate upside down over the mold. Invert the two, giving them a good shake, then lift off the mold.

Boodles Orange Fool

A specialty of Boodles Club, a gentleman's club in London's St. James'.

4 oz sponge cake, broken into pieces (about 4 cups)	⅔ cup heavy cream whipped cream and orange slices, to decorate
finely grated rind of 2 oranges and 1 lemon	
juice of 4 oranges and 2 lemons	SERVES FOUR TO SIX
⅓ cup sugar	

Arrange the pieces of sponge cake in the bottom of a glass serving dish. Stir the fruit rinds and juices with the sugar until the sugar has dissolved.

Whip the cream until thick but not stiff, then slowly whip in the fruit juice and rinds. Spoon over the sponge cakes and leave in a cool place until the juices have seeped into and soaked the sponge cakes.

Decorate with whipped cream and orange slices.

Eton Mess

The annual prize-giving at Eton College – one of England's foremost private schools – is held on June 4th. On that day, parents and pupils picnic on the famous playing fields with this luscious dish as part of their meal.

1 lb strawberries	6 meringue shells,
6 tablespoons Kirsch	crushed
2 cups heavy cream	
	SERVES FOUR TO SIX

Reserve a few small strawberries, chop the remainder and place in a bowl. Sprinkle the Kirsch over the berries, cover and chill for 2–3 hours.

Whip the cream until it stands in soft peaks. Gently fold in the strawberries and their juices and the meringues.

Spoon into a glass serving dish and decorate with the reserved strawberries just before serving.

Summer Pudding

Summer Pudding was created in the eighteenth century as an alternative to the rich pastry desserts that were then fashionable. Any combination of mixed summer red berries and fresh currants can be used.

2 lb black currants, red currants, raspberries, loganberries, strawberries, blackberries	heavy cream, or plain yogurt, to serve
about ¾ cup sugar	SERVES SIX
about 8 thin slices of bread, crusts removed	

Put the fruit in a bowl, sprinkle the sugar over, cover and leave overnight. Put the fruit and juice into a saucepan, then heat gently for 2–3 minutes. Taste and add more sugar if necessary.

Cut some of the bread into wedge shapes to fit into the bottom of a deep round 5-cup mold. Cut and arrange the remaining bread so that it lines the mold neatly with no spaces between the slices.

Fill with the fruit and most of the juice, then cover the fruit completely with a layer of bread. Spoon the remaining juice over the top layer of bread. Place a plate that just fits inside the mold on top of the pudding. Put one or more weights or cans of food on top and leave in a cool place overnight.

To serve, carefully run a knife between the pudding and the mold, then invert onto a serving plate. Serve with cream or plain yogurt.

Trifle

In eighteenth century recipes a syllabub mixture was used to cover the custard, rather than the cream, and fruit was not included.

1 cup lightly crushed amaretti cookies	*Topping*
1 cup lightly crushed macaroons	6 tablespoons sweet white wine
5 tablespoons sweet white wine	1 tablespoon Cognac freshly grated rind and
1 tablespoon orange liqueur	juice of ½ lemon
1¼ cups heavy cream	3 tablespoons sugar
vanilla bean	¾ cup heavy cream
4 egg yolks	crystallized violets and
3 tablespoons sugar	roses, to decorate

SERVES FOUR TO SIX

Mix together the first three ingredients for the topping in a bowl and leave overnight.

Mix the amaretti and macaroons in a glass bowl and sprinkle with the wine and liqueur. Leave to soak. Gently heat the cream with the vanilla bean to simmering point. Remove from the heat, cover and leave to infuse for about 20 minutes. Remove the vanilla bean.

Blend the egg yolks with the sugar. Stir in a little of the cream, then pour back into the bulk of the cream. Cook over a low heat, stirring constantly, until the sauce thickens – do not allow it to boil. Leave to cool, stirring occasionally to prevent a skin from forming, then strain over the amaretti and macaroons and leave to set.

Strain the liquid for the topping and stir in the sugar, stirring until it has dissolved. Slowly stir in the cream, then whip lightly with a balloon whisk until the topping just holds its shape. Spread over the set custard.

Cover and leave in a cool place overnight. Decorate with crystallized violets and roses just before serving.

Fruit Crumble

Fruit crumbles are high on the list of favorite English puddings. They are extremely simple to make and any type of fruit that grows wild or in the garden can be used.

1½ lb raw fruit, eg blackberries, apples, plums, rhubarb, prepared and sliced according to type	4 tablespoons hard unsalted butter or margarine, chopped
⅔–1 cup granulated sugar	⅓ cup light brown sugar custard sauce (see page 92), to serve
¾ cup all-purpose flour	
pinch of salt	SERVES FOUR

Put the fruit into a buttered ovenproof dish and add granulated sugar to taste.

Sift the flour and salt together, toss in the butter or margarine, then rub in the fat until the mixture resembles breadcrumbs. Stir in the brown sugar. Spoon the crumble over the fruit and bake in a preheated 375° oven for 25–30 minutes until the top is brown and the fruit tender.

Serve with custard sauce.

CABINET PUDDING (page 78)

Queen of Puddings

For an extra special finish to this pudding, pipe the meringue in swirls, rosettes, scrolls or a lattice design, then decorate with slivered almonds or chopped pistachio nuts and pieces of glacé or crystallized fruits.
Although not strictly traditional, dried fruits can be added (but omit the rose water) and lemon curd used instead of jam. The rose water in this version adds a medieval touch.

2½ cups milk or a mixture of milk and cream
3 tablespoons unsalted butter, diced
long strip of lemon rind
2 eggs, separated
few drops of rose water
⅓ cup sugar
1½ cups fresh white breadcrumbs

about 2 tablespoons red fruit preserves or good quality jam, warmed
slivered almonds or chopped pistachio nuts and glacé or crystallized fruits, to decorate

SERVES FOUR

Put the milk, or milk and cream, butter and lemon rind in a saucepan and bring just to simmering point. Stir onto the egg yolks in a bowl, add the rose water and half the sugar, then strain onto the breadcrumbs. Stir the lemon rind back into the mixture. Let stand for 20 minutes, then remove the rind.

Pour into a greased 5-cup ovenproof dish and bake in a preheated 350° oven for about 25 minutes until just set.

Spread the preserves or jam over the pudding. Beat the egg whites until stiff. Beat in half the remaining sugar, then gradually beat in the rest.

Spoon into a pastry bag fitted with a star tube and pipe decoratively over the pudding. Return to the oven for 15–20 minutes until the meringue is a light golden brown. Decorate with nuts and glacé or crystallized fruits.

Cabinet Pudding

This type of custard-based pudding was very popular in the eighteenth century. Richer versions use cream instead of milk, a higher proportion of cookies, and sometimes brandy is added as well.

2 cups milk
vanilla bean
3 tablespoons glacé cherries, halved
3 tablespoons chopped candied angelica
3 eggs
3 tablespoons sugar

2 slices pound cake, diced
¾ cup crushed amaretti cookies
3 tablespoons raisins, chopped

SERVES FOUR

Put the milk and the vanilla bean in a saucepan and bring slowly to a boil. Remove from the heat, cover and leave for 15 minutes.

Arrange some of the cherries and angelica in a buttered 3 cup plain mold.

Lightly whisk the eggs and sugar together. Remove the vanilla bean from the milk then stir the milk into the eggs.

Mix the pound cake, ratafias, raisins and remaining cherries and angelica together and spoon into the mold. Strain in the egg and milk and leave to soak for 15 minutes.

Place the mold in a deep baking pan, surround

with boiling water and cover with parchment or wax paper. Bake in a preheated 325° oven for about 1 hour until just set.

Remove the mold from the oven and let stand for 2–3 minutes before unmolding.

Spotted Dick

This is one of the most popular of real English puddings. When well made, Spotted Dick is light and delicious.

1½ cups fresh white breadcrumbs	finely grated rind of 1 large lemon
⅔ cup self-rising flour	1 egg, beaten
pinch of salt	4–6 tablespoons milk
6 tablespoons shredded suet	custard sauce (see page 92), to serve
⅓ cup sugar	
1 cup (6 oz) currants	SERVES FOUR TO SIX

Mix the first seven ingredients together in a bowl, form a well in the center, add the egg and sufficient milk to give a fairly soft, but not sticky, dough.

Form into a roll on a lightly floured surface, then wrap in buttered parchment or wax paper. Wrap in foil, securing the seams well, but allowing the pudding plenty of room to rise during cooking. Steam in boiling water for 1½–2 hours, checking the level of the water about every 30 minutes and replenishing with more boiling water if necessary.

Serve with custard sauce.

Castle Puddings

This is just one of the many sponge pudding recipes that are such a popular part of traditional English cooking. Folding in beaten egg whites will produce a really feather-light sponge pudding.

8 tablespoons (1 stick) unsalted butter, softened	about 3 tablespoons blackberry, raspberry or strawberry jam
⅔ cup sugar	custard sauce (see page 92), to serve
2 eggs, separated	
¾ cup self-rising flour	
pinch of salt	SERVES FOUR
few drops of vanilla extract	

Beat the butter and sugar together in a bowl until light and fluffy. Gradually beat in the egg yolks, then lightly fold in the flour, salt and vanilla extract.

Beat the egg whites until stiff, but not dry, then lightly fold into the sponge mixture. Divide the jam among eight buttered timbale molds or custard cups and divide the sponge mixture among the molds.

Bake in a preheated 350° oven for about 20 minutes until well risen and a light golden color.

Leave to stand in the molds for a minute or two before unmolding onto warmed plates. Serve with custard sauce and extra warmed jam, if liked.

Sussex Pond Pudding

Unmold the cooked pudding onto a warmed plate before serving so that, as it is cut into, the rich, buttery, lemony juices flow out to form a golden pond.

1⅔ cups self-rising flour	1 egg, beaten
pinch of salt	10 tablespoons cold
¼ cup shredded suet	unsalted butter, diced
4 tablespoons cold	¾ cup light brown sugar
unsalted butter,	1 large, thin-skinned,
coarsely grated	juicy lemon
1 teaspoon finely grated	
lime or lemon rind	SERVES SIX
4–6 tablespoons milk	

Mix the flour and salt together, then stir in the suet, grated butter and lime or lemon rind. Add enough milk to the egg to yield ¾ cup and add to the dry ingredients. Quickly mix to a soft, but not sticky, dough.

Knead lightly, then on a lightly floured surface, roll out to a 12-inch round. Cut out one-quarter of the dough in a fan shape to within 1 inch of the center and set aside. Use the remaining dough to line a buttered 1½-quart steaming mold.

Mix the diced butter and sugar together and place about two-thirds in the mold. Prick the lemon well all over with a needle and place on the butter and sugar. Pack the space around the lemon with more butter and sugar, filling the mold completely.

Roll out the reserved dough to a round 1 inch larger than the top of the mold. Dampen the exposed edge of the dough lining the mold. Cover with the lid and seal the edges together well.

Cover the top of the mold with a piece of buttered, pleated wax paper, then cover with a piece of pleated foil and secure the foil firmly with string.

Put the mold in a large saucepan with enough boiling water to come halfway up the sides of the mold. Cover and steam for 2½ hours, replenishing with boiling water as necessary.

Devonshire Whitepot

A delicious light, creamy West Country variation of bread and butter pudding.

3 slices of buttered bread,	finely grated rind of
crusts removed, cut	½ lemon
into triangles	1 teaspoon orange flower
2½ cups heavy cream	water
1 egg, beaten	⅓ cup raisins
2 egg yolks	freshly grated nutmeg
⅓ cup sugar	
	SERVES FOUR

Arrange half the bread, buttered side down, in an ovenproof dish. Place the dish in a roasting pan.

Beat the cream, egg, egg yolks, lemon rind and orange flower water together. Stir in the raisins and pour into the dish. Arrange the remaining bread on top, buttered side uppermost and sprinkle with nutmeg. Surround the dish with boiling water and bake in a preheated 350° oven for about 45 minutes until the pudding is lightly set, and the top crisp and golden.

Bakewell Tart

As with many traditional dishes there are a number of different recipes that are claimed as the genuine, authentic one. In the case of this dish, there is also a dispute about the title – whether it should be called a tart or pudding.

½ lb basic pie pastry
4 tablespoons unsalted
    butter
⅓ cup sugar
1½ eggs, beaten

¾ cup ground almonds
raspberry jam
confectioners' sugar, for
    sifting

SERVES FOUR TO SIX

Roll out the pastry on a lightly floured surface and use to line a 6-inch flan ring placed on a baking sheet. Chill for 30 minutes.

Prick the pastry lightly, cover with parchment paper and scatter a layer of baking beans over the paper. Bake blind in a preheated 400° oven for 10 minutes. Remove the baking beans and wax paper lining and return the pastry to the oven for a further 5 minutes.

Meanwhile, beat the butter and sugar together in a bowl until light and fluffy, then gradually beat in the eggs, beating well after each addition. Fold in the almonds.

Spread a thin layer of jam over the bottom of the pastry case. Remove the flan ring and fill the case with the almond mixture. Bake for about 25 minutes until the filling is just firm.

Carefully transfer the cooked tart to a wire rack and sift confectioners' sugar over the top. Serve the tart warm or leave until cold.

Christmas Pudding

This pudding benefits from 3–4 months maturing.

½ lb (2 sticks) unsalted
    butter
1⅓ cups dark brown
    sugar
3 eggs, beaten
3 tablespoons dark corn
    syrup
⅔ cup self-rising flour
pinch of salt
juice of 1 lemon
½ teaspoon each of
    ground cinnamon;
    freshly grated nutmeg;
    apple pie spice

finely grated rind of
    1 orange and 1 lemon
4 cups fresh breadcrumbs
1⅓ cups (½ lb) each of
    golden raisins; raisins;
    currants
⅓ cup (2 oz) chopped
    mixed peel
¼–½ cup brandy
brandy, for flaming
brandy butter (see
    page 91), to serve

MAKES TWO 2-LB PUDDINGS

Beat the butter until soft, add the sugar, beat until fluffy. Gradually beat in the eggs and syrup.

Sift the flour, salt and spices together, then fold into the mixture with the lemon juice, fruit rinds, breadcrumbs, fruits, mixed peel and brandy.

Spoon into two 1-quart steaming molds. Cover with a circle of wax paper then a piece of foil, pleated across the center, and securely tied in place and leave overnight.

Put the molds in a large saucepan with enough water to come halfway up the sides of the molds, cover and steam for 5 hours, then remove from the water. Leave to cool completely then cover with a clean piece of wax paper and a pudding cloth secured with string and the ends of the cloth knotted over the top of the mold. Leave in a cool place to mature before using. When required, steam for about 3 hours and serve with brandy butter.

Cakes, Buns and Biscuits

THE CAKES of England are in a class of their own, but the types that are so well-known and loved today did not begin to be made until the eighteenth century. Until then, cakes were really an extension of bread-making, with sugar, spices and dried fruits being added to make a plain yeast dough more interesting.

Modern cake-making evolved as a result of a number of different factors: the use of beaten eggs as a leavening agent, the discovery of effective chemical leavening agents, such as baking soda and cream of tartar, and the construction of enclosed cooking stoves.

Although plain cakes, gingerbreads and rather solid fruit cakes provided fare for country suppers and high teas for years, it was not until the growth of afternoon tea became fashionable among the upper classes that cakes developed into the numerous varieties and shapes and sizes that exist nowadays.

Devon Flats

These cookies are not as rich as a first glance at the list of ingredients may suggest, and they are very easy to make.

1⅔ cups self-rising flour	1 egg, beaten
pinch of salt	about 1 tablespoon milk,
⅔ cup sugar	to mix
½ cup heavy cream	

MAKES ABOUT TWENTY-FOUR

Mix the flour and salt together then stir in the sugar. Lightly bind together with the cream, egg and sufficient milk to give a fairly stiff dough. If the dough feels at all sticky, cover it and place in the refrigerator to firm up.

Roll out the dough on a lightly floured surface to about ⅓ inch thick and cut into circles with a 3-inch cutter. Transfer to a greased baking sheet and bake in a preheated 425° oven for 8–10 minutes, until a light golden brown. Carefully transfer to a wire rack and leave to cool.

The cookies can be stored in an airtight container in a cool place for up to 3 days.

Cornish Saffron Cake

Saffron was added to cakes and breads to make them look rich and buttery.

3 tablespoons sugar
½ cup warm milk
2 teaspoons active dry yeast
⅔ cup boiling water
pinch of saffron strands
3¼ cups all-purpose flour
1 teaspoon salt

8 tablespoons (1 stick) unsalted butter, diced
1 cup currants
⅔ cup chopped mixed peel

MAKES EIGHT SLICES

Butter an 8-inch cake pan. Dissolve 1 teaspoon sugar in the milk, sprinkle the yeast over the surface and leave in a warm place for 20 minutes until frothy.

Meanwhile, pour the boiling water onto the saffron in a small bowl and leave to infuse.

Sift the flour and salt together. Rub in the butter until the mixture resembles breadcrumbs. Stir in the remaining sugar, currants and peel. Make a well in the center, strain in the saffron liquid, then add the yeast liquid. Gradually draw the dry ingredients into the liquids and mix to a soft dough.

Put into the prepared pan, cover with a damp cloth and put the pan inside a large plastic bag. Leave until the dough has risen to the top of the pan. This should take about 1 hour in a warm place, 2 hours at room temperature.

Remove from the bag, uncover and bake in a preheated 400° oven for 30 minutes. Reduce temperature to 350° and bake for 30 minutes.

Leave in the pan for 2–3 minutes before turning out onto a wire rack to cool.

Madeira Cake

The best way to enjoy Madeira cake is with a glass of one of the sweeter Madeiras, as was the custom in the nineteenth century. It can also be served with a cup of coffee at mid-morning or at tea-time.

10 tablespoons unsalted butter, softened
⅔ cup sugar
4 eggs, beaten
1⅔ cups cake flour
⅓ cup rice flour
1 teaspoon cream of tartar
1 teaspoon baking soda
pinch of salt

juice of 1 lemon
strip of candied citron peel

MAKES SIX TO EIGHT SLICES

Butter and bottom line a 7-inch-round, deep cake pan with wax paper.

Cream the butter with the sugar until light and fluffy, then gradually beat in half the egg.

Sift the flour, rice flour, cream of tartar, baking soda and salt together, then fold into the creamed mixture alternately with the remaining egg and lemon juice.

Turn into the prepared pan and bake in a preheated 350° oven for 20 minutes. Open the oven carefully and lay the citron peel on top of the cake. Bake for a further 45 minutes.

Let cool in the pan for a few minutes before turning out and cooling, right side up, on a wire rack.

Muffins

To serve muffins, pull them almost apart through the center, toast them and spread with butter. Close them up and eat while still warm.

1 teaspoon sugar
1½ cups warm milk
2 teaspoons active dry
   yeast
3¼ cups all-purpose flour

1 teaspoon salt
1 teaspoon fine semolina

MAKES ABOUT FOURTEEN

Dissolve the sugar in the milk, sprinkle the yeast over the surface and leave in a warm place for about 20 minutes until frothy.

Sift all but 1 teaspoon flour and the salt together, then form a well in the center. Pour the yeast liquid into the well, draw in the flour and mix to a smooth dough.

Knead the dough on a lightly floured surface for about 10 minutes until smooth and elastic. Place in a clean bowl, cover with a dish towel and leave in a warm place until doubled in size. Roll out the dough on a lightly floured surface using a lightly floured rolling pin to about ¼–½ inch thick. Leave to rest, covered, for 5 minutes, then cut into rounds with a 3-inch plain cutter.

Place the muffins on a well-floured baking sheet. Mix together the reserved flour and semolina and use to dust the tops. Cover with a dish towel and leave in a warm place until doubled in size.

Grease a griddle or heavy frying pan and heat over a moderate heat, until a cube of bread turns brown in 20 seconds.

Cook the muffins on the griddle or frying pan for about 7 minutes on each side.

Cider Cake

A succulent, moist cake from Somerset, the cider county. Store the cake in an airtight container for at least 2 days before eating, but it will keep for much longer.

⅔ cup (4 oz) glacé
   cherries, chopped
⅔ cup (4 oz) currants
⅔ cup (4 oz) golden
   raisins
⅔ cup (4 oz) raisins
⅔ cup dry hard cider
1 cup light brown sugar

1 egg, beaten
1¼ cups all-purpose flour
3 tablespoons cornstarch
2 teaspoons baking
   powder
pinch of salt

MAKES EIGHT TO TEN SLICES

Put the fruit and the cider in a bowl and leave to soak in a cool place overnight.

Stir in the sugar and egg, then sift in the flour, cornstarch, baking powder and salt. Mix well together, then transfer to a buttered 9-×5-×3-inch loaf pan. Bake in a preheated 325° oven for 2 hours.

Leave to cool slightly in the pan, then turn out onto a wire rack and let cool completely.

MUFFINS (left)

Crumpets

Serve the crumpets toasted, preferably in front of an open fire, with butter or cheese or try them as a base for poached or scrambled eggs.

1 teaspoon sugar
3 cups warm milk
2 teaspoons active dry
　yeast
3¼ cups all-purpose flour

1 teaspoon salt
½ teaspoon baking soda

MAKES ABOUT FIFTEEN

Dissolve the sugar in 1¼ cups of the milk, sprinkle the yeast over the surface then leave in a warm place for about 10 minutes until frothy.

Sift the flour and salt into a warm bowl and form a well in the center. Pour half the yeast liquid into the well, then gradually draw the flour into the liquid using a wooden spoon and beat until smooth. Gradually beat in the remaining liquid to give a thin, smooth batter.

Beat well, then cover with a clean dish towel and leave in a warm place until the mixture has doubled in size.

Dissolve the baking soda in the remaining milk, beat it into the batter well, then leave for 30 minutes.

Butter a griddle or heavy frying pan and three 3½ inch plain metal cutters or crumpet rings.

Heat the griddle or pan and the rings over a moderate heat until a cube of bread turns brown in 20 seconds. Pour enough batter into each ring to fill them to a depth of about ½ inch.

Cook for about 4 minutes until the surface is dry and honeycombed with holes. Carefully remove the rings, turn the crumpets over and cook on the other side for 2–3 minutes. Continue until all the batter is used, greasing and heating the griddle and rings before adding the batter.

Parkin

English parkin recipes originate in the north of the country and always contain oatmeal, syrup and black treacle or molasses. They keep well and should be left for 2 or 3 days in an airtight container before being eaten.

½ cup corn syrup
½ cup black treacle or
　molasses
4 tablespoons lard, diced
4 tablespoons unsalted
　butter or margarine,
　diced
⅔ cup brown sugar
1⅔ cups all-purpose flour
pinch of salt
2 teaspoons ground
　ginger

½ teaspoon ground
　cinnamon
1½ teaspoons baking
　soda
1⅓ cups oatmeal
1 egg, lightly beaten
¼ cup milk

MAKES TWELVE SLICES

Butter and line a 9-inch square pan.

Gently warm the syrup, treacle or molasses, lard, butter or margarine and sugar together in a small saucepan until the syrups and fats have melted and the sugar has dissolved.

Sift the flour, salt, spices and baking soda together into a bowl and stir in the oatmeal. Form a well in the center, then add the egg and milk, beaten together.

Pour the warm ingredients into the milk, then gradually draw the dry ingredients into the liquids and beat to give a smooth batter.

Pour into the prepared pan and bake in preheated 350° oven for about 1 hour.

Allow to stand for about 2 minutes before turning out onto a wire rack. Leave for 2 minutes then carefully remove the lining paper. Turn the cake the right way up and leave to cool.

Store in an airtight tin for 2–3 days before eating.

Chelsea Buns

Yeast fruit buns were a specialty of the old Chelsea Bun House, Grosvenor Row, London, and are said to have been bought by, or for, King Georges II, III and IV. Serve freshly made and warm.

1⅔ cups all-purpose flour
1½ teaspoons active dry
  yeast
1 teaspoon granulated
  sugar
½ cup warm milk
½ teaspoon salt
2 tablespoons unsalted
  butter, diced
1 egg, beaten
½ cup mixed golden
  raisins, currants and
  raisins

3 tablespoons chopped
  mixed peel
⅓ cup brown sugar
3 tablespoons unsalted
  butter, melted
confectioners' sugar, for
  glazing

MAKES TWELVE

Butter an 8-inch square pan.

Sift ½ cup of the flour into a warm bowl. Stir in the yeast. Dissolve the granulated sugar in the milk and stir into the flour. Leave in a warm place for about 20 minutes until frothy.

Sift the remaining flour and salt into a warm bowl, then rub in the diced butter. Form a well in the center, pour in the yeast mixture and the egg, then draw in the dry ingredients to make a smooth dough. Knead for 10 minutes.

Place the dough in a clean bowl, cover with a clean dish towel and leave to rise for 1¼–2¼ hours until doubled in size. Knead the dough lightly on a floured surface, then roll it out to a large rectangle, about 12×9 inches.

Mix the dried fruit, peel and brown sugar together. Brush the dough with melted butter, then scatter the fruit mixture over the surface, leaving a 1 inch clear border around the edges.

Roll the dough up tightly like a jelly roll, starting at a long edge. Press the edges together to seal them. Cut the roll into 12 slices.

Place the rolls cut side uppermost in the prepared pan. Cover with a clean dish towel and leave in a warm place until doubled in size.

Bake in a preheated 350° oven for 30 minutes. Blend a little confectioners' sugar with water to make a sugar glaze and brush over the top while still hot. Leave to cool slightly in the pan before turning out.

Carrot Cake

The flavor improves if the cake is kept in an airtight container for a few days before it is eaten, but the topping should not be added until shortly before the cake is eaten.

½ lb (2 sticks) unsalted butter or margarine, diced
1⅓ cup light brown sugar
4 eggs, separated
2 teaspoons grated orange rind
1 tablespoon lemon juice
1¼ cups self-rising flour
1 teaspoon baking powder
⅓ cup ground almonds

1 cup (4 oz) chopped walnuts
4 cups grated young carrots

Topping (optional)
½ lb (1 cup) cream cheese
2 teaspoons honey
1 teaspoon lemon juice
¼ cup (1 oz) chopped walnuts

MAKES EIGHT SLICES

Butter and line an 8-inch round deep cake pan.

Beat the butter or margarine and sugar together in a bowl until light and fluffy. Beat in the egg yolks, then stir in the orange rind and lemon juice.

Sift the flour and baking powder, then stir into the mixture with the ground almonds and the walnuts.

Beat the egg whites until stiff and fold into the cake mixture with the carrots. Pour into the prepared pan and hollow the center slightly. Bake in a preheated 350° oven for about 1½ hours, covering the top with foil after an hour if it starts to brown.

Let cool slightly, then turn out onto a wire rack and remove the lining paper. Let cool completely.

Beat the cheese, honey and lemon juice and spread over the top of the cake. Sprinkle with walnuts.

Eccles Cakes

These crisp, plump, buttery pastries were once considered to be so sinfully rich that they were banned. They are named after the Lancashire town of Eccles. Serve them, still warm, as a tea-time treat.

½ lb puff pastry
¼ cup sugar
½ teaspoon apple pie spice
⅔ cup (4 oz) currants
¼ cup chopped mixed peel

2 tablespoons unsalted butter, melted
lightly beaten egg white and sugar, for glazing

MAKES TWENTY

Roll out the pastry to ⅛ inch thickness on a lightly floured surface using a floured rolling pin. Cut into circles using a 4-inch plain cutter.

Mix the sugar and spice together, then stir in the currants, peel and butter. Place 1 teaspoon of the fruit mixture on the center of each circle. Brush the edges with beaten egg white, then draw them up over the filling and pinch them together to seal. Turn the pastries over and roll lightly to flatten them slightly. Cut three parallel slits in the top of each, brush with beaten egg white and sprinkle liberally with sugar.

Place on a dampened baking sheet, and bake in a preheated 425° oven for about 15 minutes until golden brown.

Transfer to a wire rack to cool slightly before serving.

BRANDY SNAPS (page 90), CARROT CAKE (above) AND ECCLES CAKES (above)

Brandy Snaps

Brandy snaps were popular as Fairings – that is they used to be sold, or given as gifts, at country fairs. They can be kept, unfilled, in an airtight container for up to a week.

4 tablespoons unsalted butter, cubed	1 teaspoon brandy
⅓ cup sugar	finely grated rind of ½ lemon
2 tablespoons corn syrup	
6 tablespoons all-purpose flour	*Filling*
½ teaspoon ground ginger	¾ cup heavy cream
	MAKES ABOUT TWELVE

Line two or three large baking sheets with baking parchment paper.

Gently heat the butter, sugar and syrup until the butter has melted and the sugar dissolved. Remove from the heat.

Sift the flour and ginger together, then stir into the melted mixture with the brandy and lemon rind.

Drop teaspoonfuls of the mixture onto a prepared baking sheet, leaving about 4 inches in between them. Bake toward the hottest part of a preheated 350° oven for about 7 minutes until the cookies are bubbling and lacy in appearance.

Meanwhile, prepare another sheet of the mixture ready for baking. As soon as the baked cookies are cooked, remove them from the baking sheet using a spatula and roll each one around the buttered handle of a wooden spoon. Leave on the handles until set, then gently twist each one, remove it and leave to cool completely.

If the cookies set before they have been shaped, return them to the oven for a few minutes to soften.

Store in an airtight container until required.

Just before serving, whip the cream until it stands in soft peaks. Spoon into a pastry bag fitted with a star tube and pipe the cream into the snaps.

Dorset Apple Cake

This simple, delicious version of apple cake comes from Dorset and is at its best if served still warm, with custard sauce or brandy butter (see page 92) for a dessert, or plain butter for tea or with mid-morning coffee.

1⅔ cups all-purpose flour	1½ cups chopped tart apples
1½ teaspoons baking powder	1 egg, beaten
pinch of salt	milk, to mix
8 tablespoons (1 stick) unsalted butter, diced	½ teaspoon ground cinnamon
1 cup light brown sugar	
	MAKES SIX TO EIGHT SLICES

Butter and line a 7-inch round deep cake pan.

Sift the flour, baking powder and salt together. Rub in the butter until mixture resembles crumbs.

Stir in ⅔ cup of the sugar, the apple and the egg. Mix to a dough adding a little milk if too stiff.

Put into the prepared pan. Mix the remaining sugar with the cinnamon and sprinkle over the top. Bake in a preheated 350° oven for about 45–50 minutes until a light golden brown and cooked through.

Cool in the pan for 12 minutes, then turn out.

Lardy Cake

Recipes for this traditional tea-time cake originate from several counties, particularly Wiltshire, Oxfordshire and Cambridgeshire. Serve it freshly baked, warm and upside down on a warm plate, and break, don't cut the cake, into pieces.

1 cup sugar
1½ cups warm water
2 teaspoons active dry
   yeast
3¼ cups all-purpose flour
2 teaspoons salt
12 tablespoons lard

1 cup mixed golden
   raisins and currants
⅓ cup chopped mixed
   peel

MAKES EIGHT SLICES

Butter an 8-×10-inch pan. Dissolve 1 teaspoon sugar in the water, sprinkle the yeast over the surface then leave in a warm place for about 20 minutes until frothy.

Sift the flour and salt together into a bowl. Dice 1 tablespoon of the lard, toss in the flour, then rub it in. Form a well in the center, pour in the yeast liquid, then draw in the dry ingredients and mix to a dough that leaves the sides of the bowl clean.

Turn onto a lightly floured work surface and knead well for 10 minutes until smooth and elastic. Place in a clean bowl. Cover with a damp cloth, put the bowl inside a large plastic bag and leave until doubled in size. This will take about 1 hour in a warm room, about 2 hours at normal room temperature.

Turn the dough onto a floured surface and roll out to a rectangle about ¼ inch thick. Cut the remaining lard into small pieces and dot one third of it over the surface of the dough. Sprinkle it with one third of the fruit, peel and remaining sugar. Fold the dough in three, folding the bottom third up and the top third down. Give a half turn, then repeat the process twice more.

Roll the dough out to fit the prepared pan. Cover with oiled plastic wrap and a cloth and leave to rise in a warm place for 20–30 minutes until puffy. Score the top into eight rectangles, then bake in a preheated 425° oven for about 45 minutes.

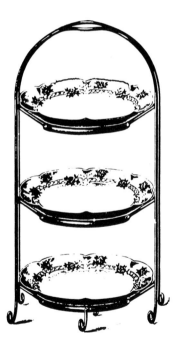

Traditional Accompaniments

OVER THE years, combinations of ideal accompaniments to complement a main dish have evolved. Some accompaniments are fairly specific, such as Yorkshire pudding to serve with roast beef. Others, such as red currant jelly, will enhance a number of different dishes.

Brandy Butter

Serve brandy butter with Christmas pudding, mince pies or with hot fruit or spicy desserts.

½ lb (2 sticks) unsalted butter, diced
1⅓ cups confectioners' sugar

6 tablespoons Cognac or other good brandy
squeeze of lemon juice

MAKES ¾ lb

Beat the butter in a slightly warmed bowl until it is smooth and light. Gradually beat in the confectioners' sugar. When most of it has been incorporated, start to gradually add the brandy, alternating with the remaining sugar, and beat until the sauce is light and fluffy. Beat in the lemon juice.

Pile into a cold bowl, cover and refrigerate to allow the flavors to mature before serving.

Custard Sauce

This is traditional English custard which can be served hot, warm or cold with all manner of puddings. If it is to be served cold, cover the surface closely with plastic wrap to prevent a skin from forming.

2½ cups milk or mixture of milk and cream
1 vanilla bean
about 2 tablespoons sugar

4 egg yolks, beaten

MAKES 2½ CUPS

Gently heat the milk, or milk and cream, with the vanilla bean to just below simmering point. Cover, remove from the heat and leave to infuse for 15 minutes. Remove the vanilla bean.

Blend the sugar and egg yolks, then gradually stir in the milk, or milk and cream. Pour into a clean saucepan and heat gently, stirring, until the sauce thickens enough to coat the back of the spoon. Do not allow to boil.

Red Currant Jelly

Red currant jelly can be served with any lamb, game or even chicken dishes.

3 lb red currants
2½ cups water
sugar

Place the currants in a preserving kettle with the water and simmer gently for about 30 minutes until the fruit is very tender.

Spoon the fruit into a scalded jelly bag or triple thickness of cheesecloth attached to the legs of an upturned stool, and leave to drain into a clean bowl. Leave to drip undisturbed without squeezing the bag or cloth as this would make the jelly cloudy.

Measure the liquid, pour it back into the pan and add 1 lb (2⅔ cups) sugar for each 2½ cups liquid. Heat gently, stirring with a wooden spoon, until the sugar has dissolved. Bring to a boil and boil rapidly for 10–15 minutes or until setting point is reached.

To test for setting point, drop a tiny amount of the jelly onto a cold saucer, leave to cool, then push the jelly with a finger. If the surface of the jelly wrinkles, setting point has been reached. Remove the pan from the heat while carrying out the test.

Pour into warmed, sterilized jars, and put wax disks, wax side down, on the surface of the jelly. Cover immediately with a dampened round of wax paper. Store in a cool place.

Bread Sauce

This is the traditional accompaniment to roast chicken, turkey and game.

1½ cups milk
½ onion, stuck with
  2 cloves
½ bay leaf
3 black peppercorns
1 blade of mace
6 tablespoons fresh white
  breadcrumbs

salt
1 tablespoon unsalted
  butter
about 2 tablespoons
  heavy cream (optional)

SERVES FOUR

Bring the milk to a boil with the onion stuck with cloves, the ½ bay leaf, peppercorns and mace. Remove from the heat, cover and leave to infuse for 30 minutes.

Strain the milk, then bring to simmering point. Gradually stir in the breadcrumbs, then simmer for 3 minutes, stirring. Season and stir in the butter and cream, if using. Serve as soon as possible.

Cumberland Sauce

Cumberland sauce is served cold as a traditional accompaniment to all manner of game dishes, both hot and cold. It will keep for several weeks if stored in a covered glass jar in the refrigerator.

1 large lemon	sprinkling of ground
1 large orange	ginger
⅔ cup water	6 tablespoons tawny port
⅔ cup red currant jelly	wine
1 teaspoon Dijon mustard	
salt and pepper	MAKES ABOUT 1½ CUPS

Using a potato peeler, thinly pare the rind from the orange and lemon, avoiding the pith.

Cut the rind into very fine strips, then place in a small saucepan with the water. Bring to a boil and simmer for 5 minutes. Drain and refresh under cold running water.

Squeeze the juice from the fruit and strain into a bowl. Stir in the jelly, mustard and seasoning and place the bowl over a saucepan of hot water. Heat, stirring, until the jelly has melted. Stir in the port and fruit rinds and continue to heat until the sauce begins to thicken.

Pour into a dish or into a glass jar if the sauce is to be kept.

Index